May 29th 1991

Dear Dad,

You must check out pages 140 thru 145, my how things changed!!

Happy Birthday

Love
Greg.

OLD QUEENS, N.Y.

IN EARLY PHOTOGRAPHS

❧

BY

Vincent F. Seyfried

AND

William Asadorian

❧

DOVER PUBLICATIONS, INC.
New York

ACKNOWLEDGMENTS

In the course of research and the compilation of materials for this book, the authors drew upon the invaluable assistance and the picture collections of a number of individuals and organizations. Grateful acknowledgment is hereby made to the following: Robert F. Eisen; Robert C. Friedrich; the Greater Ridgewood Historical Society; George P. Miller; the Nassau County Museum Reference Library; Robert Presbrey; The Queens Borough Public Library, Long Island Division; The Queens Historical Society; Fred Rodriguez; the Suffolk County Historical Society; Edward B. Watson; Charles F. J. Young; and Ron Ziel.

Published in Canada by General Publishing Company, Ltd., 30 Lesmill Road, Don Mills, Toronto, Ontario.
Published in the United Kingdom by Constable and Company, Ltd., 3 The Lanchesters, 162–164 Fulham Palace Road, London W6 9ER.

Old Queens, N.Y., in Early Photographs is a new work, first published by Dover Publications, Inc., in 1991.

Manufactured in the United States of America
Dover Publications, Inc., 31 East 2nd Street, Mineola, N.Y. 11501

Edited by Alan Weissman
Book design by Carol Belanger Grafton, CBG Graphics

Library of Congress Cataloging-in-Publication Data

Seyfried, Vincent F.
    Old Queens, N.Y., in early photographs / by Vincent F. Seyfried and William Asadorian.
        p.   cm.
    Includes index.
    ISBN 0-486-26358-4
    1. Queens (New York, N.Y.)—Description—Views. 2. New York (N.Y.)—Description—Views. 3. Queens County (N.Y.)—Description and travel—Views. I. Asadorian, William. II. Title.
F128.68.Q4S49   1991
974.7′1—dc20   90-36358
                                                                        CIP

INTRODUCTION
Queens: A Historical Overview

Physical Features

Queens County lies on the western end of Long Island, extending fourteen miles from the East River on the west to Lakeville Road at the Nassau border on the east, and fifteen miles from Long Island Sound on the north to the Atlantic Ocean on the south. Queens is the largest of the boroughs of New York City. As large as Brooklyn and the Bronx together, the borough accounts for 37 percent of the territory of the city. It also has the most waterfront, facing on the East River, Newtown Creek, Long Island Sound, Jamaica Bay and the Atlantic Ocean.

Queens, like all the rest of Long Island, was formed when the last glacier ground its slow way down over New England, pushing masses of earth and rubble under it and before it out into Long Island Sound. When the glacier of the last Ice Age retreated some 14,000 to 12,000 years ago, the farthest southern advance was marked by a high ridge, or terminal moraine (Harbor Hill), which extends east and west along the middle of Queens and Nassau (as well as much of Kings and Suffolk) Counties. The melting waters from this ridge created a flat outwash plain that today is the gently sloping southern half of the island. The Interboro Parkway and Grand Central Parkway east of Kew Gardens follow the crest of the ridge. Buried ice masses, after melting very slowly, left collapsed pockets, called kettles, here and there, some of which filled up with water and created ponds. About 6,000 years ago, the alpine vegetation of the Ice Age yielded to the first trees, with oak the dominant species.

The highest points in Queens are on the crest of the moraine, some 170–190 feet above sea level in Cypress Hills Cemetery and Forest Park, and 200–206 feet on the Grand Central Parkway above Queens Village.

The soil of Queens is perhaps the richest on Long Island, with clay, gravel and silty loam in different areas; as you go east on Long Island the soil becomes increasingly thin and sandy, ending in the pitch-pine and scrub-oak cover of eastern Long Island. Nineteenth-century agriculture benefited from the long growing season: 172 to 200 days, the longest in New York State.

The Indians

Long before the coming of the first Europeans, Queens was the home of various Indian tribes belonging to the Algonquian peoples. The Indians were attracted to sites along the coasts that offered abundant fresh water, timber for building and natural shelter from winter storms. Finds of Matinecock Indian artifacts have turned up on the banks of Newtown Creek, particularly at its headwaters; in East Elmhurst along Flushing Bay; and in College Point and Flushing bordering Flushing Bay. Jameco artifacts have been found along the meadowlands adjoining Jamaica Bay. Inland sites were less hospitable, although Beaver Pond in Jamaica early attracted Indian settlement. The numerous bays and creeks around Queens provided fin fish (eels, herring, haddock) and shellfish (oysters, clams, crabs, mussels) in abundance, and the primeval forests of the interior offered a variety of game and migratory fowl for both food and clothing. The numerous thickets provided natural foods like strawberries, grapes, chestnuts and walnuts, and grouse and quail nested on the ground. The Long Island Indians, unlike some others, were a peaceful lot, living in small bands; they had progressed to an agricultural way of life. Two of their crops were corn (maize) and squash. The Indians had long ago learned that a cultivated plot soon becomes exhausted, and crop rotation was accomplished by burning down a patch of woods and moving to a nearby site. The Indians of Queens County left three names on the land in Queens: Jamaica, named after the Jameco Indians; Rockaway, named after the Reckowacky Indians; and Maspeth, supposedly meaning "place of bad water."

The Dutch and New Amsterdam

The first provable discovery of New York harbor was made by Henry Hudson, an Englishman in the employ of the Dutch East India Company, who sailed into the bay on his ship, the *Half Moon*, on September 3, 1609. In 1614 Adriaen Block and Hendrick Christiaensen, also sailing under the aegis of the Dutch East India Company, built a fort and some buildings at the tip of Manhattan. Block passed through Hell Gate with his vessel and so was the first European to see Queens and, incidentally, to realize that Long Island was indeed an island.

The Dutch sent out further settlers, and Peter Minuit, the first director general, purchased Manhattan from the Indians in 1626. Peter Stuyvesant came as governor in 1637, and between that year and 1656 he made periodic grants of land on the Queens shore to individual Dutchmen; these were the "out plantations." It seems likely that the nominal owners stayed in Manhattan and entrusted the running of their Queens acres to tenants or managers, who worked the farm with laborers.

While New Amsterdam was taking shape, English colonists began to drift south from the older Massachusetts colonies into Connecticut; they founded New Haven in 1639, and in 1640 a group crossed Long Island Sound and founded

Southold; in the same year another group founded Southampton. Other English groups moved westward through Long Island, and by 1644 they had founded Hempstead. The reasons for all this mobility were various: some felt a natural restlessness and desire for adventure; the constant religious bickering in the colonies moved others to migrate; still others wanted land.

It was not long before groups of English began to drift westward into Queens and into the areas under Dutch control. The first organized group of English led by the Reverend Francis Doughty formally petitioned Governor Kieft in 1642 for a grant of land at the headwaters of Newtown Creek at Maspeth. The Dutch were willing to grant a charter, provided the English would swear an oath of allegiance to the Dutch government, take a Dutch name for the colony and accept the Dutch form of government. In return they received generous terms, including the power to erect towns and the right to elect a slate of citizens from whom the Dutch would make appointments to political and civil posts. Taxes were payable at the rate of one-tenth of the crops, with no tax on gardens or orchard. Magistrates could hear petty civil cases; jurisdiction at the provincial level was reserved to the Dutch.

In 1643 a skirmish between the Indians and the Dutch in Manhattan erupted into a war, and the Indians began to raid the settlements; the Doughty settlement at Maspeth was invaded and destroyed. This setback, however, did not stop further attempts at settlement elsewhere. In 1644 Heemstede (Hempstead) was founded, and in 1645 Flushing was settled under a Dutch name—"Vlissingen"—and under Dutch governmental forms.

Ten years after the Maspeth disaster its colonists made a new attempt, this time at an inland site safe from Indian raids. The new settlement, named Middelburgh and located at what is now the junction of Queens Boulevard and Grand Avenue, Elmhurst, was founded in 1652. Because it represented a new attempt at colonizing, the inhabitants informally called it "Newtown." Governor Stuyvesant delayed in issuing a formal grant to Newtown, so the settlers bought 13,000 acres from the Indians with their own money.

The last English settlement under the Dutch was Jamaica in 1656. The authorities in New Amsterdam gave it the name "Rustdorp." Seemingly the first attempt at settlement had been on Long Neck or Old Town Neck on the shore of Jamaica Bay, but by the time the Dutch authorized the establishment in 1656, the colony had moved inland to the more favorable site of Beaver Pond.

Friction developed very early between the English and their Dutch masters; some of the causes were cultural, others political. There was first of all the difference of language, plus the strong sense of national pride in the English. The Dutch chose to live on isolated farmsteads, whereas the English tended to stick together and found communities. The Dutch had no notion of representative government, and this rankled the English colonists in the sensitive areas of taxation and the framing of laws. In the Dutch view this was proper paternalism; to the English it was despotism.

The breakout of the Anglo-Dutch War of 1652–54 had no local repercussions, but it did tend to fan the suspicion of each group for the other. In the wider world, there was intense rivalry between Dutch and English traders for the fur trade in Connecticut and the upper Hudson Valley, and English policy worked constantly to undermine Dutch relations with the Indians. The Dutch in Holland even suggested enlisting the Indians against the English if the New Englanders threatened New Amsterdam.

In Flushing, the Dutch governor Stuyvesant arrested John Bowne, a Quaker settler, for religious sectarianism, and even imprisoned him. Bowne refused to pay the fine and was sent to Holland for judgment. The directors wisely decided to free him and proclaimed religious toleration for all Protestants in the colony. Bowne's protest at his arrest has become famous as the "Flushing Remonstrance."

By the end of Dutch rule the nuclei of the three future towns (townships) of Queens County had already been established: Newtown, embracing all northwestern Queens; Flushing, all northeastern Queens; and Jamaica, all southern Queens. The settlers were largely young and moved often, either because of a desire for a safer, more economically favorable location, because of religious strife or because of friction with family or neighbors. Each settler got a piece of land and all had access to the commons; everybody farmed but many practiced skilled trades on the side (carpentry, masonry). Barter took the place of scarce money; arbitration was the means of settling all disputes in the absence of police or army.

English Rule

Dutch rule in New Amsterdam was brought to an abrupt end in August 1664, when four English vessels with a small force of men aboard under Captain Richard Nicolls seized New Amsterdam in the name of James, Duke of York, to whom King Charles had patented all Dutch lands. Nicolls proceeded to reorganize the political administration of the colony. New Amsterdam was renamed "New York" and Long Island became "Yorkshire." The whole colony of Yorkshire was divided up on the English model into "ridings" or thirds. Suffolk became the "East Riding"; the Towns of Flushing, Jamaica and what is now Nassau County became the "North Riding"; and Brooklyn, the Town of Newtown and Staten Island became the "West Riding." Captain Nicolls also promulgated a new legal code known as "the Duke's Laws," named English-style officials, such as sheriffs and overseers, and set up the courts at Hempstead.

The English colonists in Yorkshire were of course pleased to be ruled by their own countrymen, but it soon became evident that English rule was as dictatorial as Dutch rule. The settlers protested in 1669 and again in 1674 at their lack of representation, and the duke at last consented to convene a Provincial Assembly at Hempstead in October 1683, to address grievances. The result of this was the appointment of a new governor, Thomas Dongan, and the setting-up of a permanent Provincial Assembly to which the colonists would send delegates. More important was the abolition of the riding system and the creation of ten counties, three on Long Island and seven in the Hudson Valley. On November 1, 1683, Queens, Kings and Suffolk Counties officially came into existence; the counties, in turn, were divided into "towns." In Queens County there were five towns: Newtown, Flushing, Jamaica, Hempstead and Oyster Bay. Jamaica was made the county seat. All the colonists were granted a "Charter of Liberties," which went far to meet the demand for representation. Two years after the historic assembly of 1683, the Duke of York ascended the throne of England as King James II.

Queens County in the seventeenth century benefited from a stable and growing society. Persons who had secured patents from the Dutch were able to confirm them with the new regime by the payment of a quitrent. People in humble circumstances usually owned a house lot in a village, plus a wood patch for firewood and a sliver of meadowland for salt hay. A sizable proportion of the population was landless, and these had to rent quarters and hire themselves out as farm laborers or set up as artisans (blacksmiths, carpenters, masons). There were few rich people, for wealth at this time simply meant more land and a wider variety of everyday goods. Some people—25 percent in 1698—owned slaves purchased in New York. Similarly, there were few destitute people—the family took care of its own. Almost everyone farmed and a few carried on trades on the side. Coined money was rare and barter satisfied everyday wants. Marriage was in a sense the cement of society; it united families and was taken seriously; divorce was extremely rare in colonial life; interestingly, over a third of the people of Newtown married more than once. The Dutch and the English almost never intermarried; the two societies co-existed but kept apart socially, the English attending their Congregational churches and the Dutch their Reformed kirk.

Life in the Eighteenth Century

Government in the eighteenth century began to respond to the increasing complexity in social life. Many new officials appear for the first time: assessors, collectors, supervisors, trustees, fence viewers, highway surveyors, highway over-seers. Taxes increased to pay for the new offices and the roads and bridges, and levies were assessed to pay for English wars. In Newtown the average townsman paid a week's wages yearly in taxes, which were payable in money or goods.

Society was changing as the population increased. The Dutch were beginning to integrate into the social fabric, and their names appear for the first time as officeholders; the younger generation spoke English and the use of Dutch slowly declined. Workingmen became more numerous, although free labor was in constant competition with slaves and indentured servants. New craftsmen appeared: brewers, vintners, clerks, weavers, coopers. The number of wealthy persons increased, to judge from wills. Wealth now was not just in land but also in livestock, fowl and a broad variety of crops and tools. For the first time bonds and mortgages appeared as assets. Slaveholders rose from 25 percent of the people in 1698 to 32 percent a few years later. Status consciousness appeared; in earlier times most people had been "yeomen," i.e., farmers; now a justice called himself "Esquire," and well-off persons considered themselves "gen-tlemen." Women seem not to have risen much in the social scale; they seldom inherited land in wills and had to be satisfied with life tenancy, inheriting only personal property. Longevity is difficult to establish; roughly 70 percent of the men and 50 percent of the women reached the age of 60.

Religion continued to be a divisive force. In 1702 the English government attempted to impose the established church (Anglican) on the New York province. The English colonists were then Congregationalist (with rule by local congregation) or Presbyterian (with rule by authoritarian synod). Queen Elizabeth had spent her long reign (1558–1603) systematically stamping out Catholicism and organizing an English version of the old faith with herself as supreme head. Many of her subjects, however, in embracing the new Protestantism, insisted on the same right to fashion a new religion that Elizabeth had assumed, and, in their reforming zeal, went on to dump not only dogmas but the hierarchy as well. Elizabeth shrewdly saw that if it could be argued that the people needed no religious heads like cardinals or bishops the same could be said of civil heads, and thus her own

position could be endangered. She therefore bitterly fought the reformers and insisted on the retention of a formal hierarchy of bishops. Those who refused to accept the Anglican system fled to America. When the government in 1702 imposed a tax on the New York province to pay the salaries of Anglican ministers, and even seized dissenters' churches, the colonists rebelled. The government proved stronger and extorted the tax, but for years the colonists obstructed the Anglican clergy and used every evasion to withhold payment. The colonists—typical Americans—val-ued religion but not conformity.

The Quakers, when they first appeared, were even more intensely unpopular. They insisted on public witness in the form of singing, shaking, speaking in tongues and fainting. By 1725, however, they had ceased public exhibitionism and become conventional. The Quakers were strong in Flushing, Maspeth, Westbury, Gravesend and Westchester. They were notable for policing each other's conduct and did not hesitate to admonish weaker brethren. They married only among themselves and arbitrated all disputes privately.

The first sign in Queens that the frontier days were over came when the land ran out. The common land had largely been sold off by 1750 and private land became harder to obtain. Wills indicate that the price of land doubled between 1690 and 1725. Landholders, to avoid fragmentation, left their estates to the eldest sons and only money or personal property to younger ones. The result was that young men and their families moved out to New Jersey and Westchester, where land and farms were still unlimited.

The Revolution

The American Revolution was really thirty years in the making; it represented the accumulated resentment growing out of a whole series of aggressions on the part of the British Parliament despite repeated, forceful protests of the colo-nists. Parliament saw itself as the ultimate source of law and authority, and fully expected the colonies to accept its mandates as dutiful and obedient subjects. The colonists had chafed against Dutch and later ducal rule because both denied them a voice in their own government; now Parlia-ment was brushing off their demands to manage their own affairs. Trouble began in the 1740's, when the tax rate rose to pay for King George's War (1744–48) and then the Seven Years' War (1755–1763). Towns were forced to provide men and goods besides. New taxes were laid on quitrents, slaves, wigs, services and liquor. Taxes rose about sevenfold by 1757 and fourteenfold by the 1760's to pay for war-related costs: coastal lookouts, barracks, bedding, food, candles. The burden was beginning to strain the local resources. On top of this, French-Canadian refugees, prisoners, soldiers and war-wounded increasingly became public charges. The Quarter-ing Act of 1765 requiring colonists to house and support British troops added to the growing colonial resentment. Parallel to the new taxes were regulations in 1764 imposing duties on American products and restricting the freedom to trade, all designed to protect the economy of the mother country. When a storm of protest rose over the restrictions, and the colonists began to boycott British goods, Parliament backed down, but as a symbol of its right to tax, retained the tax on tea. The result was the Boston Tea Party, where some Americans, disguised as Indians, seized the tea and dumped it in the harbor.

On September 4, 1774, a Continental Congress, com-posed of delegates from all the colonies, convened at

Philadelphia to consider measures of resistance. In New York the local delegates drew up a list of grievances and urged residents to declare themselves, but Queens County refused to send any delegates. Opinion was sharply divided; many viewed the Congress as disrespectful and illegal; a minority urged action. In December 1774, local meetings held at Newtown and Jamaica reiterated their allegiance to King George but censured Parliament for oppressing the colonies. The speakers emphasized the right of every man to private property and to its disposition and to the principle that only elected assemblies had the power to tax. In January 1775, a letter signed by 56 leading Queens men disowned these resolutions and condemned the Congress. In April 1775, when the question arose to send delegates to a second Continental Congress, Queens County again declined.

The crucial year was 1775. On April 19, the first armed skirmish between British troops and American colonists broke out at Lexington and Concord. Opinion was beginning to harden; in earlier years the colonists had felt a pride of identification with British nationality; now a sense of American identity was beginning to form out of common interests and against a common aggressor. In Queens, the Towns of Flushing, Jamaica, Hempstead and Oyster Bay were strongly Tory; only Newtown in western Queens was somewhat Patriot in sentiment. In Jamaica, a poll of county delegates voted three-to-one against sending delegates to any "rebel" Congress and they threatened to gather arms and ammunition to oppose the United Colonies.

The New York Convention of November 20, 1775, summoned the 26 most prominent Loyalists to appear before it, and, when they refused, appointed Colonel Heard and his New Jersey Militia to disarm the Loyalists and to arrest the most vocal among them. Colonel Heard crossed the Astoria Ferry on January 19, 1776, and scoured Newtown, searching farmhouses and confiscating arms. The Colonel secured a pledge from some Loyalists to remain neutral; 19 of the 26 cited to appear in New York were arrested and sent to Philadelphia, where they were paroled and allowed to return home.

In March 1776 it was decided to arrest all active Tories to prevent the British from using Queens as a friendly port of debarkation. A small Patriot force moved through Newtown on March 6 and Jamaica on March 7. In Newtown (Astoria and Elmhurst), 193 patriots were enrolled into a militia; Jamaica could furnish only 30 men. All in all, 10,000 cartridges and 1,000 flints were gathered. A strong effort was made to win over the Tories to the rebel cause.

Excitement reached a high point in Queens when the news was received that the general congress at Philadelphia, on July 4, 1776, had dissolved the old connection with England and declared the colonies free and independent. When the document was publicly read in Elmhurst the next day, it created a sensation; many were unprepared for so radical a step and felt that the colonists had gone too far; others were fired with enthusiasm.

Britain was determined to put down the rebellion and landed troops on Staten Island. The Continental Congress ordered that all the livestock on western Long Island be collected and driven eastward out of reach of the British Army. Forty-four men under General Nathaniel Woodhull undertook to round up the cattle at the moment that the British Army was landing in force in South Brooklyn (New Utrecht). Washington and the American Army were entrenched on Brooklyn Heights. On the morning of August 27, 1776, Washington, under cover of fog, retreated with his forces over the East River to New York, and so avoided a decisive battle with the superior British forces. General Woodhull, meanwhile, drove off all the livestock he could find in Newtown through Jamaica toward Hempstead. The news of the surrender of Long Island to the British demoralized Woodhull's men, who deserted to return to their own now-endangered farms. Woodhull himself delayed a day at Jamaica and, as a result, fell into the hands of British raiders at Carpenter's Tavern in Hollis (at what is now Jamaica Avenue and 197th Street). Woodhull refused to say "God Save the King" at British demand and received several saber cuts in a scuffle that followed. He was sent to a British prison ship in New York harbor and later died of his wounds.

The British lost no time in occupying all of Queens County. Outriders occupied the high ground at Cypress Hills and Forest Park, and on August 28 took over Jamaica; Flushing fell on the 29th. The British, under the impression that the American General Lee planned to encircle them by crossing over from Manhattan to Astoria, quickly marched inland with Major General Robertson at their head. Moving along Flushing and Grand Avenues, they reached Elmhurst and set up camp between Corona Avenue and Queens Boulevard (for convenience, the later names of the streets are used here). General Robertson, taking a part of the army, quickly marched along Broadway, Woodside, and Newtown Avenue, Astoria, to Hell Gate. Finding no trace of Generals Lee or Washington here, he stayed for two weeks and built a battery on high ground.

On September 15, 1776, Robertson sent a detachment of his troops over to Manhattan but took his main force along the shoreline (now 20th Road) to Flushing and then to Whitestone, where he crossed over to Westchester. By October 12 the combined British and Hessian forces evacuated Astoria altogether and followed Robertson to Westchester. On October 28 the British and American forces met and fought the Battle of White Plains.

The British forces left in Elmhurst, Jamaica and Flushing now dug in for a long-term occupation under the command of Sir William Howe. Howe took over the Renne house at what is now the corner of Queens Boulevard and 57th Avenue for his headquarters and wrote out a long report to Parliament about the Battle of Long Island. A sizable concentration of British troops was encamped in tents all along 39th Avenue from Woodside Avenue to Queens Plaza (now largely the Sunnyside Yards). The officers were billeted in the stone houses of the Dutch farmers in the area.

The divided loyalties of the American colonists became evident during the occupation. The Tories rejoiced at Washington's defeat and showed their loyalty by wearing a red ribbon tied around their hats or a red flannel cloth tucked in their hatbands. They brought foodstuffs to the quartermaster and informed on the patriots. The rebels had either been clapped in prison or abandoned their farms to join the American Army. To buy favor, the Tories professed their loyalty in a petition addressed to General Howe, dated October 21, 1776.

British records reveal the disposition of the various occupying forces. The King's American Regiment, 80th Grenadiers and the 38th and 54th Regiments garrisoned Flushing. Jamaica in central Queens was secured by the Light Dragoons, the Irish Volunteers, DeLancey's Brigade and the 64th Company of Grenadiers reinforced with two Hessian regiments. Midway between Flushing and Jamaica, on 73rd Avenue (old Black Stump Road), Fresh Meadows, was a large encampment of soldiers. In St. John's Cemetery in Middle Village were stationed the 42nd Highlanders. The Royal Highland Regiment was posted in Jackson Heights along the now-vanished Trains Meadow Road; the 17th Light Dragoons occupied camps along the Head of the Vleigh Road, near the site of Queens Borough Hall. In the camps along 39th Avenue, Dutch Kills, were the Royal Artillery and Lord Cornwallis' 39th Regiment.

Life was hard for the soldiery, who lived in tents in summer and sod huts in winter; the officers forced themselves as unwelcome guests on neighboring farmers and often chose the warm kitchen for their quarters. The farmers had to endure petty thefts and the insolence of their own slaves, who lost respect for their masters when they saw them humiliated by their British guests. Respect for the British was demanded: an American had to tip his hat or hold it under his arm when meeting or addressing a British officer.

The British Army lived off the country and forced the Americans to sell their foodstuffs at fixed prices; if the farmer refused, his stock was confiscated. The demand for firewood was insatiable, and foraging parties constantly combed the countryside cutting down trees and even fences to provide wood to heat the sod huts. The enforced requisition of rye, corn, wheat and vegetables made foodstuffs scarce and often the farmers had hardly enough food for their own families. Harsh, cold winters like that of 1779 brought misery to the local inhabitants and a scarcity of staples. The primeval forest cover was rapidly disappearing to the foraging parties and by the end of the occupation hardly a trace remained.

British soldiers controlled all movement over the roads. A pass signed by an officer was required to ride a horse or drive a wagon to market; a pass was equally necessary for boats transporting produce to New York and no sailing at all was permitted at night. Movement even with a pass did not protect the farmer from seizure of his horse or wagon at the demand of some quartermaster with the excuse of military need. These high-handed actions aroused hatred, but resistance was impossible.

The British seized all the few public buildings for their own purposes. In Elmhurst (then Newtown) the Presbyterian church on Queens Boulevard near Grand Avenue had its steeple sawed off and was then demolished for lumber for huts. The Dutch Reformed church on Broadway was converted into a powder magazine. The Episcopal (Anglican) church survived because it was the Church of England and the British officers and men prayed here on Sundays for the king and the success of British arms. The Friends' Meeting House in Flushing saw use as a prison and army hospital.

For the colonists the most painful part of the occupation was the thievery of the soldiers. Although farmers kept firearms and guarded their barns at night, stealing of property was rampant. The only law was the law of the occupiers, and although Generals Howe and Clinton made the gesture of issuing proclamations against thievery, officers and non-commissioned officers alike winked at complaints of theft. The civil courts were suspended during the occupation, closing another avenue of redress. The presence of a British officer in a farmhouse was a small deterrent against theft, for it meant that a sentry walked post in front of the house. A British officer was also required by military regulations to pay twenty shillings a week for his board, making his presence somewhat more bearable.

The Americans fought back with guerilla tactics, conducting raids on British stores and weapons. To check them the British raised a local militia of Loyalists and refugees under General Oliver DeLancey. This ragtag force soon earned a reputation for lawlessness and thievery. On the other side, the "whaleboat men"—New Englanders authorized by American commanders to raid British shipping in Long Island Sound—struck terror into British hearts because of their boldness, their mastery of the terrain and their ability to appear and then vanish seemingly at will. The whaleboaters thrived on raiding British shipping and military stores and seizing both soldiers and Loyalist sympathizers for ransom or exchange. To combat them, a British guard ship was stationed off Riker's Island, and guard detachments were posted on shore at Astoria, East Elmhurst and Whitestone.

The defeat of General Cornwallis at Yorktown in October 1781 ended British hopes of winning the war. The British delayed pulling out their troops until they could evacuate the Loyalists of Queens County, who now rightly feared retribution. In 1782 the Loyalists were shipped off to exile in Nova Scotia, Canada. Evacuation day for the army of occupation finally came in 1783. The Flushing and Elmhurst contingents marched along Woodside Avenue and the route of the Brooklyn–Queens Expressway to Penny Bridge at Calvary Cemetery and then into Bushwick. The Jamaica troops formally marched out on November 25, 1783, under the watchful eye of the patriots lined up along Jamaica Avenue. On the night of December 8, 1783, a patriotic celebration was staged at what is now Parsons Boulevard and Jamaica Avenue, and in every window thirteen candles were lighted to celebrate the birth of the new thirteen-state nation.

Although the British were physically gone, the damage they left behind them took years to obliterate—the ruined houses, the ravaged woodlands, the destroyed churches. In addition, there was the bitterness of divided families and the feeling of neighbor against neighbor. The resentment against the more flagrant Loyalists culminated in the confiscation of their property in 1785. Many Tories passed their last days in exile in far-off Nova Scotia rather than returning to Long Island to face the angry hostility of their fellow townsmen.

Queens in the Nineteenth Century

The quietest era of Queens history was the first fifty years after the Revolution. The disruption in social and economic life, the physical damage to farms and woodlands and the general neglect into which roads, mills, etc., had fallen left Queens in an exhausted condition from which it took decades to recover. The population remained almost static, and development slowed to a snail's pace. The onset of the War of 1812 touched Queens County only lightly; the fear of an enemy invasion motivated the Federal government to build coastal defenses around New York harbor. When the British attempted to surprise and burn Sag Harbor in a night raid, Washington responded in 1814 by building Fort Decatur, a blockhouse at what is now Beach 137th Street in Rockaway, and Fort Stevens, a stronger stone fort in Astoria at 1st Street and 26th Avenue. Neither of these fortifications ever saw enemy action, for in 1815 the war came to an end.

Beginning about 1800, turnpike fever hit Queens County. This was a revolution in transportation that affected much of the eastern seaboard. The idea was to privatize the public roads—to lease them for fixed periods to private companies, which would be authorized to collect tolls and in return maintain good road surfaces. In March 1801 the Flushing & Newtown Turnpike was incorporated; in 1806, the Jamaica and Rockaway Turnpike; in 1809, the Jamaica & Brooklyn Road Company; in 1812, the Hempstead and Jamaica Turnpike; in 1814, the Williamsburgh & Jamaica Turnpike; and, in 1816, the Newtown & Bushwick Turnpike. In the 1830's, after a twenty-year lapse, additional companies came along, until finally there were 19 operating wholly or partly in

Queens. The turnpikes were very important in the history of Queens because speedy overland travel became possible for the first time. Stagecoach companies sprang up and began operating fixed routes between Manhattan and Brooklyn and the villages of Queens using the improved turnpike roads.

Another exciting development in this era was the building of the first racetracks. Queens was rural and offered an abundance of flat, open surfaces ideal for horse racing. In 1821, the Legislature authorized the Union Course, a track just south of Jamaica Avenue and between 78th and 85th Streets, Woodhaven. In 1825, the Eclipse (later Centerville) racetrack came along south of Rockaway Boulevard and east of Woodhaven Boulevard. These two tracks operated for almost fifty years and their existence stimulated travel, a local hotel industry and settlement along Jamaica Avenue. The lithographs that Currier & Ives and their imitators produced of stirring races and track scenes at the Union grounds made Queens known not only along the eastern seaboard but in the antebellum South, where horses and horse racing were much esteemed. The Metropolitan Jockey Club (later Jamaica Race Track) and the Queens County Jockey Club (later Aqueduct Race Track) came at the end of the century (1894) with larger grounds and more modern grandstands.

In 1847 Albany passed a piece of legislation entitled "The Rural Cemetery Act," which was destined to have the most profound effect in Queens. Down to 1847 interment of the dead had been limited to three choices: burial in a churchyard, on one's farm or in a town cemetery. By midcentury the natural growth of population, increasing immigration from Ireland and Central Europe, and a shortage of open land in Manhattan and Brooklyn forced consideration of a change. The new legislation commercialized death for the first time by authorizing corporations to buy land, open cemeteries and sell plots for money to private individuals. Within the next five years cemetery corporations began to buy up farms in Queens County and lay out large cemeteries: Calvary (1846), Evergreens (1848), Cypress Hills (1852), Mount Olivet (1852), St. Michael's (1852) and Lutheran (1852). In later years all of these expanded their acreage and many new cemeteries (Catholic and Jewish) sprang up, especially in the Town of Newtown.

Perhaps the most notable event in these years before the Civil War was the slow growth in the old colonial villages and the appearance on the scene of real-estate promoters. Jamaica, a hamlet in colonial days, was incorporated as a village in 1814, and Flushing followed in 1839. These two had already been town seats for 150 years and were now raising their status; Newtown Village (today's Elmhurst) remained a hamlet and did not become populous enough to attain incorporated-village status, although it was the oldest of the three.

Astoria was the first in a long line of new settlements founded by one man or a realty company. Stephen Halsey, a fur trader, along with several associates, founded Astoria in 1839 and promoted and enlarged it over thirty years. In 1834 Charles and Peter Roach acquired the Long Island City shoreline and, beginning in 1848, developed Ravenswood into the first "Gold Coast" on Long Island, a neighborhood of large riverfront mansions. In 1840 Middle Village began as a refreshment stop for farmers at the midpoint of Metropolitan Avenue. It was a long haul for farm wagons from the Williamsburgh ferries to Jamaica, and the hotel and cottages provided a welcome break. Woodhaven began as a real-estate promotion in 1835; Queens Village, in 1837; Maspeth, in 1852; Winfield, Corona and College Point, in 1854. All of these were very small places at first but, once the

seed had been planted, they grew into substantial villages. Not all promotions were successful: Winantville, Columbusville and Flammersburg have disappeared from the map.

The pre–Civil War era closed with the appearance of a few fledgling enterprises that would later grow great. The Long Island Rail Road opened its road from Brooklyn to Jamaica on April 18, 1836; by 1837 the new road had reached Hicksville and by 1844 the end of the island. The railroad greatly stimulated southern Queens and opened Woodhaven and Jamaica to the outside world. This era saw the first stirrings of industry in Queens: a turpentine refinery at Astoria opened in the 1830's, a carpet factory in the '40's and a small shipyard in 1838.

The Civil War itself had little impact on Queens. Few men volunteered at first and not until the draft of 1863 was the war felt. Jamaica reacted with draft riots and the burning of government stores; Flushing and Newtown (Elmhurst), with a tradition of local militias, sent small detachments of men; College Point responded with a company of recent German immigrants. There was no Queens industry to profit from the war, and the distant battles in the South and West were scarcely heard of in the rural villages of the county. The only mementos of Civil War participation that survive in Queens today are the monument in front of the Flushing Town Hall and the graves of the volunteers in Flushing Cemetery.

The post–Civil War years, in contrast with the war years, were a period of unparalleled growth in Queens. The stimulus that the war gave to industry, transportation and society in general helped to break up the tendency to parochialism and stagnation characteristic of many rural areas. People moved about more, and in Queens County this translated itself into the creation of new villages. In 1869 Richmond Hill was developed; in 1868–69, Glendale. In 1872, the "German Settlement" of inner Astoria was laid out by the Cabinet Makers' Union; in 1870, William Steinway, the piano manufacturer, founded a whole industrial complex at Bowery Bay; and in 1872–73, Bayside was extensively boomed by promoters. Queens Village got the same treatment in 1871–72. South Flushing was pushed in 1872–73 by that tireless Queens promoter, Benjamin W. Hitchcock, a sheet-music publisher, who, in a thirty-year career, developed Woodside (1867), Corona (1874), Ozone Park (1882), Hammels (1884) and Union Course (1892). Ridgewood sprang up in 1881, Hollis in 1885 and Morris Park in 1884.

By the 1890's the land was running out. As villages expanded, they began to touch and then grow into each other. This process was greatly stimulated in Queens by the building of the street railways, which had first appeared in 1865 and by the '90's had become a network. By the turn of the century, eastern Queens—the old Town of Flushing—was the last major unsettled area of open farmland.

The 1890's were an era of consolidation—not only social and geographical, but political as well. The idea of a Greater New York had been growing—the merging of Manhattan, the Bronx, Staten Island and western Long Island (Queens and Brooklyn) into a metropolis. In 1890 the State set up a commission to study the idea, and in 1894 the people were asked to express their opinion in a nonbinding ballot. The historic vote occurred on November 6, 1894. Manhattan favored the idea; in Queens, Long Island City and the Towns of Jamaica and Newtown voted in favor, but Brooklyn vetoed the proposition, as did the Town of Flushing, by 1407 to 1144. In March 1896, the Legislature passed the Consolidation bill, and Governor Morton signed it on May 11. All the old town governments went out of business on December 31,

1897, and on January 1, 1898, the Greater City became a legal fact.

Queens in the Twentieth Century

The years from 1898 to World War II might be summed up as the "Era of Urbanization" of Queens on every front. The first twenty years were a period of tremendous infilling, adding greatly to the population density. A record number of new communities were founded, many of them of limited geographical extent because of the rapid exhaustion of available land. In the area of the old Town of Newtown only three new communities arose, all clustered around the headwaters of Flushing Creek: Forest Hills in 1906 (north of Queens Boulevard), and Forest Hills Gardens (below Queens Boulevard) and Kew Gardens in 1912. The old Town of Jamaica was less thickly settled and offered more sites. Here were founded St. Albans (1892), South Ozone Park (1907), Laurelton (1906) and Howard Beach (1911). The old Town of Flushing was still largely open land and easily accommodated Auburndale in 1901, Beechhurst in 1907 and Malba in 1908. The border with Nassau, which was all farmland, provided sites for Bellerose in 1897 and Bellaire in 1908. Swamp and meadowland in the watercourses of the now-vanished Train's Meadow and Horse Brook, long considered undesirable for building, were filled in and became the sites for Jackson Heights (1907–1920's) and Rego Park (1923). The Rockaway peninsula gave rise to Belle Harbor and Neponsit, both in 1908.

The most momentous event in the history of Queens occurred in 1909 when the long-planned Queensboro Bridge finally opened, ending the century-old isolation of the county and the old dependence on ferries. The bridge dead-ended in a marshy area of Long Island City and, to realize its tremendous potential, the city began to plan and build an arterial highway from the bridge exit through the heart of Queens to Jamaica. The new six-mile highway was pieced together from the former Thomson Avenue and Hoffman Boulevard and laid out as a 200-foot-wide thoroughfare, the widest in the city. The name chosen for the road aptly described it: Queens Boulevard.

One of the major changes in this era, greeted with mixed emotions by residents of Queens, was the changing of all the street names to a uniform numbering system. Many of the older villages like Long Island City and Elmhurst had used their own local numbering systems; many others had used identical historical and botanical names, resulting in a proliferation of Washington and Lincoln Streets along with Oak, Beech and Pine Streets. The Philadelphia numbering system, proposed in 1911 and adopted in 1915, numbered streets consecutively from west to east and assigned numbered avenues from north to south. In many places the attempt to harmonize existing streets to a new pattern was difficult and forced many modifications. Arterial streets retained their names, as did diagonal streets that defied inclusion in a grid pattern. The result today is that Queens streets run from numbers 1 to 271 west to east, and from numbers 1 to 165 north to south.

One of the major factors in the development of Queens suburbs in this era was the revolution in transportation. In 1900 the Pennsylvania Railroad took over the Long Island Rail Road and immediately made plans to electrify it. A huge power plant was erected in Long Island City, and on July 26, 1905, the first electric train ran from Brooklyn to Rockaway Beach. In August electric service opened to Jamaica and in December to Valley Stream; in May 1908, service opened to Hempstead. Fast, frequent train service made it possible for the first time for commuters to live in the suburbs and work in New York; this proved a tremendous stimulus to home-buying in Forest Hills, Kew Gardens, Jamaica, Hollis, Queens Village, St. Albans and Springfield. The opening of the Pennsylvania Station and East River tunnel in September 1910 added direct through railroad access to midtown Manhattan.

The extension of rapid transit to Queens followed shortly. In June 1915 the Interborough Subway opened to Long Island City and to Queensboro Plaza in 1916. Within a year the tracks were extended, to Astoria on February 1, 1917, and to Corona on April 21. Tracks were laid on the Queensboro Bridge and in July 1917 Second Avenue elevated trains began running to Queensboro Plaza. In central Queens the Brooklyn Rapid Transit Company extended the Myrtle Avenue elevated line to Metropolitan Avenue in 1906 and the Broadway line to the same terminus in 1914. In southern Queens the Fulton Street elevated was built east along Liberty Avenue to Lefferts Boulevard, Richmond Hill, in 1915, and, finally, the Broadway elevated was extended all along Jamaica Avenue to 168th Street, Jamaica, in 1916–18. Nothing in the whole history of Queens so profoundly affected growth and residential patterns as the coming of the rapid-transit network and its five-cent fare. Farms and open areas vanished almost overnight, and endless rows of new streets and one-family houses began to spread out into every corner of Queens.

The appearance of the airports was another part of the transportation revolution. Glenn Curtiss Airport opened on the site of the former North Beach. Purchased by the city, it became the second municipal airfield in 1939, when it was renamed La Guardia Airport. After World War II Idlewild International Airport arose on the former marshes of Jamaica Bay (1948; after the assassination it was renamed Kennedy International).

The great Depression, beginning with the stock-market crash of 1929, was not felt in Queens until 1932; the crash effectively ended the overheated building boom of the '20's. However, even in the dark days of the 1930's, some progress was made. In 1933 the Grand Central Parkway was completed between Kew Gardens and the Nassau line, and in 1935 the Interboro Parkway opened between East New York and Kew Gardens. These parkways became even more valuable when the Triborough Bridge was completed in 1936 and the Bronx-Whitestone Bridge in 1939.

The World's Fair of 1939–40 went a long way toward pulling Queens out of the Depression; more important, it thrust Queens into international prominence and acted as a showcase for both the county and the city. Great numbers of visitors came to the Flushing-Corona meadows to see the site of the fair, and benefited from the just-completed bridges and highways that made access easy. World War II, breaking out in Europe in 1939 and for us in 1941, put an end to a busy era.

The Postwar Years

The forty years since World War II represent a continuation of the great progress of the 1930's on almost every front. This is particularly true in the field of education. Queens College opened in 1937 on the spacious grounds of the former Parental School; in 1955 St. John's University moved from its Brooklyn home to occupy the former Hillcrest Golf Course in

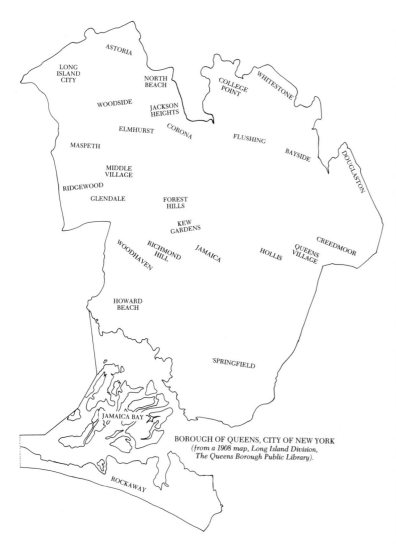

BOROUGH OF QUEENS, CITY OF NEW YORK
*(from a 1908 map, Long Island Division,
The Queens Borough Public Library).*

construction of the Long Island Expressway in successive stages from 1955 to 1960 through the heart of Queens. Even at this moment of writing the roadway is being widened to eight lanes in each direction through Maspeth, Elmhurst and Corona. The opening of the Throgs Neck Bridge in January 1961 proved the capstone to this ambitious program of transportation integration.

In 1964 and 1965 the World's Fair returned to its old site on the Flushing-Corona meadows, bigger and better than ever and with dazzling technological marvels achieved through twenty years of scientific progress. Again Queens played its role as showcase for the world; attendance was heavy during both seasons, and again several striking structures were left behind at the site as enduring monuments of the memorable event.

Certainly one of the most important and visible changes in the long history of Queens, one that will endure for long years to come, has been the ethnic transition of the 1970's and '80's. On July 1, 1968, Congress enacted a major restructuring of the immigration statutes that for the first time relaxed restrictions on immigration from third-world countries. New York, as the major port of entry for the country, immediately felt the result of this change in policy. The last twenty years have witnessed a flood of newcomers from Central and South America and the Caribbean and Asian countries, principally China, Korea, Japan, the Philippines and India. The new arrivals have tended to settle in clusters in particular neighborhoods. Flushing is now predominantly Asian; Jackson Heights and Woodside, Hispanic; Corona, Dominican; Rego Park, Hispanic and Asian; Elmhurst, Colombian and Asian; Springfield Gardens, Caribbean. European immigration has complicated the picture: Astoria is heavily Greek; Forest Hills, Israeli-Russian. When we add to all this the older overwhelming black presence in South Jamaica, St. Albans, Hollis and Cambria Heights, we see an astonishing multiethnic, multicultural county, undreamed-of as recently as 1940.

Side by side with the ethnic change of the last twenty years, and no doubt one of its effects, has been the accelerating change in the nature of housing. The single-family house in Queens has been on the decline at least since 1950. The heavy pressure of population—now roughly 1.8 million—has triggered not only multiple housing in the shape of garden and high-rise apartments, but also a disturbing tendency on the part of realtors to buy up one-family houses and erect two or three units where one house stood before. Land has become more and more valuable and the pressure to overbuild has become a problem of our time. In the commercial field, Queens is currently witnessing the construction of its first true skyscraper—fifty stories—in Long Island City.

VINCENT F. SEYFRIED

Jamaica. A postwar development was the emergence of the community college as part of the city effort to provide higher education for all. In 1960 Queensborough Community College opened on the grounds of the former Oakland Golf Course in Bayside. York College opened in 1967 in temporary quarters; the new central buildings in the heart of Jamaica were dedicated with much fanfare in 1987; finally, LaGuardia Community College opened its doors in 1971 in Long Island City in remodeled buildings once occupied by the White Motor Company.

The arterial network, so auspiciously started in the 1930's, was pushed energetically in the postwar years. The Queens Midtown Tunnel was thrown open to use in 1940. In the same year Robert Moses finished the Belt Parkway through Queens, following the Queens–Nassau border and the shore of Little Neck Bay. The final triumph was the

CONTENTS

MASPETH

1

Maspeth is the site of the first European settlement in Queens County. In 1642 the Reverend Francis Doughty obtained a charter from the Dutch authorities in New Amsterdam for a tract of land at the head of Newtown Creek at what is now Maspeth, but the outbreak of an Indian war in 1643 scattered the colony. Settlement thereafter was by individuals who found their way from Bushwick in Brooklyn and from Long Island City shore and the Dutch Kills area. The present-day village of Maspeth grew up as a result of the Maspeth Avenue and Toll Bridge Company (1836) and the Newtown and Maspeth Plank Road Company's (1801) building through the area and creating traffic—farmers' wagons and stagecoaches. In 1852 two farms were cut up into streets and building lots, opening the area from 59th Place to 69th Street and from 55th Drive south to the Plank Road, now Grand Avenue. Mount Olivet Cemetery bought up seventy-two acres in 1851. Maps show 56 houses in 1852, 135 in 1859 and 166 in 1873. Development thereafter was rapid: 1,449 residents in 1875 and 4,300 in 1898.

Maspeth today is a busy shopping center, with stores lining the length of Grand Avenue. Private houses predominate on the side streets but on the west end toward Newtown Creek there is much light industry. The population has traditionally been Polish and Italian and has remained relatively stable over the years.

1. MAURICE'S WOODS, ca. 1900. Maurice's Woods was the name given by Maspeth old-timers to a 72-acre forested tract bounded by what was to become Maurice Avenue, 66th Street, Jay Avenue and the Long Island Expressway. James Maurice, a very prominent New York lawyer, moved to Maspeth in 1840 and built a mansion on the south side of Maspeth Avenue about 800 feet west of the railroad tracks. In 1850 he was elected to the Assembly and in 1852 to Congress. In 1882 he donated the Woods to the Episcopal church as a site for a seminary, but the moving of the diocesan see to Garden City put an end to the project. For years the woods were enjoyed as a park and nature preserve by Maspethites, while houses grew up on all sides. Finally in October 1920 the church sold off the tract for development, and by 1922 streets and houses had wiped out all traces of the former green oasis. (*Courtesy of The Queens Borough Public Library, Long Island Division.*)

2. ST. SAVIOUR'S CHURCH, RUST STREET, ca. 1900. St. Saviour's Protestant Episcopal Church is bounded by 57th Road, 57th Drive, 58th Street and Rust Street in a one-acre park all its own. In 1846 James Maurice donated the hilltop site and in 1847 the little wooden rural church was built, with nothing but farms surrounding it. The rapid development of Maspeth in the 1890's transformed it into a village church. By World War I days, the neighborhood had become industrial, with warehouses, gas stations and commercial plants. On December 21, 1970, three twelve-year-old boys set fire to the church, and the tower, vestibule and ceiling were destroyed. The congregation, aided by many gifts from near and far, rebuilt the church, and it continues today to minister to the community. *(The Queens Borough Public Library.)*

3. CLINTON MANSION, OLD TOWN DOCK ROAD, 1905. DeWitt Clinton's historic mansion was bounded by 56th Drive, 56th Terrace (Old Town Dock Road), 56th Avenue and 58th Street. Built about 1725, the house was occupied by Sir Henry Clinton, the British commander, during the Revolution because it commanded a good view of the British fleet, which normally wintered in Newtown Creek, and was near the terminus of the British military road to the north shore.

DeWitt Clinton lived here on and off in the 1790's; he was Mayor of New York from 1803 to 1815 and Governor of New York State from 1817 to 1823 and from 1825 to 1828. In 1810, while living in Maspeth, Clinton was appointed a member of the Erie Canal Commission; in 1816 he headed the commission, and while governor in Albany worked to get the Erie Canal completed. It opened in October 1825. Much of the planning for New York's famous waterway was done in this house. In later years the mansion became a farmhouse, then a boardinghouse for farmhands, and finally burned down in 1933. *(Photo by Charles Van Riper; Van Riper collection.)*

4. SEWING FACTORY, ca. 1905. Women workers sewing dresses in a shop. A motor shaft running under the worktables operates the sewing machines on top. Folding gas lamps hang on long pipes from the ceiling to within a foot of the tables for the use of each seamstress. *(Stines collection.)*

5. DRAFTEES BOARDING GRAND AVENUE TROLLEY, JUNE 24, 1918. An unusual scene—soldiers drafted for World War I with their well-wishing relatives crowd about the Grand Avenue trolley car that is to transport them to the Brooklyn staging area and ultimately to Camp Upton for training. Mount Olivet Cemetery entrance is at the left. *(The Queens Borough Public Library.)*

OFF FOR
PTON.
UNE 24-18

6

6. CLINTON AVENUE, ca. 1910. A Maspeth side street. Note the unpaved streets and the absence of curbs and street lights. *(From a postcard; The Queens Borough Public Library.)*

7. GRAND AVENUE, MARCH 12, 1929. Looking east from 71st Street. The traffic is unusually light and the cars few. *(N.Y.C. Dept. of Highways; Vincent F. Seyfried collection.)*

8. GRAND AVENUE, APRIL 24, 1932 (LOOKING NORTHEAST FROM 68th STREET). The big Maspeth depot at the right that for more than sixty years housed Grand Avenue and Flushing Avenue trolleys and buses was torn down for the building of the Long Island Expressway through Maspeth in 1952. All the stores at the left have disappeared for the same reason; the buildings in the middle still survive. *(Photo by Frederick J. Weber; Weber collection, Long Island Division, The Queens Borough Public Library.)*

Clinton Ave., Maspeth, L. I.

9

7

9. GRAND AVENUE, APRIL 24, 1932 (LOOKING WEST FROM 68th STREET). The trees, the old wooden buildings and the trolley tracks have all disappeared. The Long Island Expressway was to cross under Grand Avenue in the foreground. *(Photo by Frederick J. Weber; The Queens Borough Public Library.)*

10. GRAND AVENUE, OCTOBER 7, 1934.
Looking west from Brown Place. The passage
of years since this picture was taken has made
profound changes. The Long Island Expressway now passes under the corner, having
forced the demolition of the corner buildings
at both right and left. The trolley car yielded
to buses on July 17, 1949, and most of the little
small-town-style wooden stores pictured here
have been displaced by modern successors.
*(Photo by Frederick J. Weber; The Queens
Borough Public Library.)*

6   Maspeth

11

FLUSHING

Flushing, along with Elmhurst and Jamaica, is one of the three colonial villages in Queens. In 1723 Flushing became known as the home of the first commercial nursery in America, and George Washington made a special trip in 1790 to see it. In the nineteenth century Flushing became the favorite residence of many prominent New York businessmen, who built handsome and impressive mansions along the residential streets east of Main Street. The village grew greatly in population and in the 1870's was served by three railroads. By 1900 Flushing had expanded into new outlying suburbs: Ingleside, Broadway, Queensborough Hill. Flushing today preserves four buildings from its past: the Bowne House of 1661 (the oldest in Queens), the Quaker Meeting House (1694), Kingsland (1774) and Flushing Town Hall (1863). Downtown Flushing is the shopping center for northeastern Queens and the terminus of the number 7 rapid-transit line. Main Street contains the second-largest concentration of high-rise apartment houses in Queens, and its stores reflect the increasing influx of Asian peoples since World War II.

11. FLUSHING INSTITUTE, NOVEMBER 24, 1860. The oldest dated photograph of Flushing that has survived, showing the students of the Flushing Institute lined up for a field hockey game. James Buchanan is in the White House and the Civil War has not yet started. The Institute was housed in a magnificent 1828 Greek Revival building on the east side of Main Street and just north of the New York, Flushing and North Side Railroad (later part of the Long Island Rail Road). For years prominent families of Long Island, New York and even South America sent their sons here to be educated. The school closed in 1902 and the grand old building was torn down in 1925. *(From a stereoscopic view; J. Rodriguez collection.)*

12. MAIN STREET, ca. 1870. Looking north from the railroad tracks. It is hard even to imagine that Main Street ever looked like this; today the street is thronged with people, the subway terminal at Main Street attracts crowds of commuters every morning and evening, and buses and automobiles fill the roadway from curb to curb. St. George's church, built in 1854, is the sole familiar landmark in this old-time scene. *(Stereoscopic photo by D. C. Smith; J. Rodriguez collection.)*

13. LATIMER HOUSE, LATE NINETEENTH CENTURY. This unpretentious frame house at 137-53 Holly Avenue was for the last 23 years of his life the residence of Lewis Howard Latimer (1848–1928), an inventor (most notably of an improved light-bulb filament), an expert on electric-lighting systems and a founding member—the only black member—of the Edison Pioneers, a distinguished society of Thomas Edison's early associates. Latimer had also worked for Alexander Graham Bell and Hiram Stevens Maxim. Scheduled for demolition in 1988, the Latimer house was saved by various concerned citizens and organizations with the special cooperation of Borough President Claire Schulman and at the urging of one of the present authors (William Asadorian). Now a museum, it has been relocated to a field at Leavitt Street and 34th Avenue in another part of Flushing. *(Latimer collection, Long Island Division, The Queens Borough Public Library.)*

14. LEWIS HOWARD LATIMER, ca. 1868. This, one of the few surviving photos of the inventor (from a carte de visite in his personal album), shows the young Latimer around the time he was a draftsman for a firm of patent attorneys. *(The Queens Borough Public Library.)*

15. FLUSHING BRIDGE, OCTOBER 24, 1902. This wobbly one-lane structure, built in 1892, would last till replaced in 1906 by a larger and more modern span. Note the sign: "Driving over this bridge faster than a walk is forbidden under penalty of the law." Flushing, seen in the rear, is still a rural village. *(N.Y.C. Municipal Archives.)*

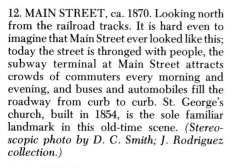

13

14

FAS... OVER THIS BRIDGE
... AN A WALK IS FORBIDDEN
... PENALTY OF THE LAW
TR... CARS MUST GO SLOW

16. L.I.R.R. STATION, SEPTEMBER 5, 1910. The Flushing railroad station, looking east. The gates protect Main Street and its traffic, and under the canopy is a glimpse of 41st Avenue. Steam trains still provided service at this time, which explains the water tank and the standpipe at left. Ahead is the one-block tunnel under the grounds of the Flushing Institute; the school in 1864 refused to let the trains go through the property without cover because the locomotive would distract the pupils' attention from their lessons! The first electric trains, using the new Main Street overpass, began running on October 21, 1913. (*L.I.R.R. photo; Robert Presbrey collection.*)

17. BROADWAY (NORTHERN BOULE-VARD) AT LAWRENCE STREET (COLLEGE POINT BOULEVARD), JUNE 25, 1912. The wooded property at the left was the Prince homestead. The Prince family established the "Linnaean Nurseries" in 1723, the first commercial nursery in America. the house was built in 1780 and survived into the 1930's. Ahead are the crossing gates for the Whitestone Branch of the Long Island Rail Road and the Bridge Street station. The steelwork for the high-level bridge over Flushing Creek now darkens this corner. In 1936–37 Northern Boulevard was widened to 150 feet at this point. (*L.I.R.R. photo; Robert Presbrey collection.*)

18. MAIN STREET FROM BROADWAY, LOOKING SOUTH, APRIL 1920. Flushing's first theater, the Janice, which opened November 24, 1914, is at the left. Main Street is in transition here: many old wooden stores and some majestic old street trees survive but the automobiles are getting numerous and the store signs more noticeable. *(Photo by Frederick J. Weber; The Queens Borough Public Library.)*

19

19. HEPBURN'S PHARMACY, 1931. The interior of Flushing's best-known drugstore in 1931. Mr. Alex Hepburn is at left, with two of his clerks. Flushing is in the depths of the Depression and prices are low. Plastic has not yet driven out tin and cardboard in packaging, labels are plain and to the point, the *Ladies' Home Journal* is only fifteen cents, and two cents will pay the postage on a letter. *(Vincent F. Seyfried collection.)*

20. MAIN STREET AT L.I.R.R. OVERPASS, DECEMBER 23, 1934. Loew's Prospect Theatre can be seen ahead; it opened about 1930 and closed in 1987, a victim of home video-tape players. The Flushing-Ridgewood trolley is waiting to make its return trip to Ridgewood. At the left can be glimpsed the new library and the white pillars of the Post Office. *(Photo by Frederick J. Weber; The Queens Borough Public Library.)*

21. MAIN STREET FROM 40th ROAD, LOOKING NORTH, DECEMBER 30, 1934. The effects of the opening of the subway in 1928 are evident here. The quaint old wooden buildings are all gone, six-story commercial structures have made their appearance, and parking is already a problem. Keith's movie palace is at the head of the street. *(Photo by Frederick J. Weber; The Queens Borough Public Library.)*

22. LOOKING DOWN NORTHERN BOULEVARD, MARCH 22, 1939. *(Photo by Frederick J. Weber; The Queens Borough Public Library.)*

22

20

WHITESTONE

Legend has it that Whitestone got its name from a big white rock offshore where the tides from the East River and Long Island Sound meet. The first settlers arrived about 1645 and built scattered farmsteads. An old fort built in the French and Indian War and rebuilt by the British formerly stood at the foot of 160th Street. For a brief time the hamlet bore the name Clintonville, but in 1854 it reverted to Whitestone. In 1854 John D. Locke, a pioneer tinware manufacturer, came to Whitestone and built a stamping mill; many of his workers followed him from Brooklyn. Stores, hotels, saloons, etc., sprang up rapidly; by 1855, the village numbered 630 people, and by 1880, 2,550. Later, wealthy New Yorkers began to build mansions along the shore. The arrival of the railroad in 1869 further boomed Whitestone. In 1906 Beechhurst was developed and quickly attracted theater and screen personalities. Today Whitestone is a prime residential community, while Beechhurst has sprouted large apartment houses along the East River shore.

23. WHITESTONE POINT, ca. 1905. A great glacial rock offshore at Whitestone Point; this rock or one like it supposedly gave the village its name. (R. Blazej collection; The Queens Borough Public Library.)

24. POST LIGHT, TIP OF WHITESTONE POINT, ca. 1905. A flashing beacon light gave warning in good weather and the bell did the same in periods of heavy fog. The whole structure sits atop a masonry wall and four brick supports. Similar lights were operated by the Coast Guard at Hell Gate, Riker's Island and Flushing Bay. (From a postcard; Vincent F. Seyfried collection.)

25. BEECHHURST, 1906. Developer's sketch of the Beechhurst shore as published by the Shore Acres Realty Company in 1906. At the far right is the Whitestone Landing Long Island Rail Road station, with what is now 154th Street in front of it. Riverside Drive curves along the shore, with 157th Street inland. Terminating at the shore is 158th Street, with the Beechhurst Yacht Club alongside. Marking the edge of the subdivision at the far left is 160th Street. A ship-repair forge works had to be cleared away before the smooth shoreline shown here could be achieved. (From a postcard; Vincent F. Seyfried collection.)

24

Bird's-eye View of Beechhurst, L.I.

BEECHHURST

30678

26

27

26. JOHN HELFRICH'S LANDING HOTEL, ca. 1907. This building still stands at 152nd Street and 6th Road. The broad porch, railings and wirework signs are all gone, as well as the restaurant and hotel facilities, but the bar survives. In pre-Prohibition days the Landing was the mecca for political outings. Steamers and barges brought the clubhouse faithful from New York and Brooklyn, who, after debarking, spent the day at nearby John Stimmel's (later Duer's) picnic grounds, baseball field and dancing pavilion till darkness brought an end to the festivities. *(From a postcard; Vincent F. Seyfried collection.)*

27. 18th STREET (NOW 14th AVENUE) FROM 8th AVENUE (150th STREET), ca. 1908. This was the central business district and the railroad was a block to the left. Every building in sight is of wood-frame construction, and hitching posts line the street. There is a gas lamp down the street and an arc light overhead. *(Vincent F. Seyfried collection.)*

28. L.I.R.R. STATION, ca. 1908. Whitestone Landing railroad station between 7th and 9th Avenues and just west of 154th Street. The site is now occupied by a Waldbaum's supermarket. When the railroad first came to Whitestone in 1869, it terminated at 150th Street; in 1886 the road was extended via a deep cut north to the waterfront. A brick roundhouse and shop were built at the water's edge and a long dock constructed for the wintering and repair of Long Island Rail Road ferries and Sound steamers. The Whitestone Branch of the railroad was abandoned on February 15, 1932. *(From a postcard; Vincent F. Seyfried collection.)*

29. BEACH, 1909. This bathing beach, just west of 147th Street, fronted the ten-acre estate of H. DeWitt Smith. The Smith estate is now Francis Lewis Park. The Whitestone Bridge would be built just around the point at the right. *(From a postcard; Vincent F. Seyfried collection.)*

30. 8th AVENUE (150th STREET), LOOKING SOUTH TOWARD 18th STREET (14th AVENUE), ca. 1912. The trolley came to Whitestone in August 1910 but lasted only ten years. At the right is Gerson's Unique Theatre; a little beyond behind the gas lamp is the First National Bank, built in 1907. The two frame houses on the left beyond the fence became the Whitestone Savings & Loan in 1932. *(From a postcard; Vincent F. Seyfried collection.)*

31. THE LANDING, FOOT OF CLINTONVILLE STREET, LOOKING EAST, JULY 1917. In the 1880's and 90's excursion parties landed here; later McWilliams Brothers operated a waterside ship's store, furnishing yacht and tug supplies. Farther east was the Long Island Rail Road dock where ferries and steamboats were repaired and wintered. *(From a postcard; Vincent F. Seyfried collection.)*

32

32. BRONX-WHITESTONE BRIDGE UNDER CONSTRUCTION, SEEN FROM WHITESTONE POINT, JANUARY 15, 1938. The bridge opened on April 29, 1939, after only twenty-three months of construction. It is by general consent one of the most beautiful of modern bridges, thanks to its clean lines, absence of pretentiousness and simplicity of design. (*Photo by R. Blazej; The Queens Borough Public Library.*)

33. STATE HISTORICAL MARKER, 7th AVENUE AND 151st STREET, 1945. This sign, now vanished, indicated the approximate site of Francis Lewis' house, burned down by the British in retaliation for Lewis' support of the American cause. Supreme Court Justice Colden, father of Queens College and a descendant of the last Royal governor, stands at the right. (*The Queens Borough Public Library.*)

33

ELMHURST

Elmhurst began more than 300 years ago when the Maspeth colony, devastated by Indians, moved inland in 1652 to safer ground at what is now Queens Boulevard and Broadway. The English colonists, required by the Dutch authorities to take a Dutch name, called the place Middelburgh. New Amsterdam fell to the English in 1664, and in 1683 Queens was reorganized on the English model into a county and five "towns." Middelburgh became the village of Newtown, the seat of the Town of Newtown; here were located the town hall, jail, tax office and town clerk's office. Farmers came from miles around to vote, to go to the three churches clustered here and to shop. Newtown slept through most of the nineteenth century but life quickened with the coming of the railroad in 1854 and the horsecar line in 1876. In 1896 Cord Meyer bought up some farms and began his high-class housing development along Elmhurst and Whitney Avenues; it was he who lobbied in Washington to change the village name to Elmhurst in 1897. The opening of the subway in 1936 destroyed many of the village landmarks but vastly stimulated local growth. Today Elmhurst is a busy, thickly populated community and a favorite with recent Oriental immigrants.

34. "OLD NEWTOWN VILLAGE, 1850." Elmhurst—then Newtown Village—in 1850, as depicted in a primitive-style painting now at The Museums at Stony Brook. Broadway is in the middle of the view and curves off to the upper left. Justice Street continues to the right. In the foreground is what became Queens Boulevard; Grand Avenue has not yet been put through. Two buildings in this view survive: the 1735 Old Episcopal Church, at 51st Avenue and Broadway, and the Reformed Church, at the corner of Corona Avenue and Broadway. (*From a painting in the collection of The Museums at Stony Brook, Stony Brook, N.Y.*)

35. ST. JAMES CHURCH, ca. 1900. The oldest surviving building in Elmhurst, the original St. James Protestant Episcopal Church, built in 1735 at what became the southwest corner of 51st Avenue and Broadway. The interior was finished in 1740; it was rebuilt in 1760 and again in 1816. During the Revolution British officers and men worshipped here. The church still possesses its original land deed and its charter from King George III. The last service was held here on June 16, 1848, after which the congregation moved across the street. Today the building is used by the Boy Scouts. (*From original glass-plate negative by Charles Van Riper; Van Riper collection.*)

38

36. OLD JAMAICA ROAD (NOW QUEENS BOULEVARD), LOOKING WEST, 1903. The vantage point is from what is now 55th Avenue. Today Queens Boulevard is ten lanes wide and every structure in the picture has disappeared, including the 1787 Presbyterian church and adjoining graveyard. Commercial buildings and apartment houses fill the area, and the "E" and "F" subway trains rumble underneath. (*Long Island Savings Bank collection.*)

37. DUTCH REFORMED CHURCH, ca. 1910. The original Reformed Church on this site, built in 1733, had been octagonal in shape with a high-pitched roof; the British used it as a powder magazine in the Revolution. It was taken down in September 1831, and the present structure was completed in July 1832; it was enlarged in 1851, and new pews and windows were installed in 1874. The chapel was built in 1858. On the Corona Avenue side is a burial ground with many gravestones of the oldest Queens families; one Dutch-inscribed stone still survives. (*Photo by Charles Van Riper; Van Riper collection.*)

38. 95th STREET AND 41st AVENUE, MARCH 24, 1926. A typical ad for new two-family homes. By the mid-1920's, land was getting increasingly scarce in western Queens, and two- and three-family homes began to predominate. It is hard for us to believe today that homes were ever so cheap or that $2,000 was acceptable for a down payment. Today, the closing costs alone would exceed that sum! (*From the* Long Island City Star.)

JAMAICA

Jamaica, along with Flushing and Newtown (Elmhurst), is one of the three villages dating back before the American Revolution. Settled in 1656 by Englishmen from Hempstead, Jamaica grew up along the now long-vanished Beaver Pond and the Indian path along the foot of the terminal moraine leading to Brooklyn Ferry—now Jamaica Avenue. The English early made it the colonial capital of Queens County with the county court and the county clerk's office. The supervisors of the five towns met here and Grace Church was the "official" government church. British troops occupied Jamaica all during the Revolution. From the end of the Revolution down to the Civil War, Jamaica remained static; real development came only in the 1870's when side streets began to be laid out. The coming of the elevated in 1916–18 triggered an enormous growth; by 1925 Jamaica Avenue from 160th to 168th Street had the highest assessed valuation in the county and it became the premier shopping center for all central Queens. After World War II Jamaica began to lose its commercial preeminence to the suburbs and to Elmhurst, but it still supports a large retail trade.

---

39. KING MANSION, ca. 1900. The King mansion (or "King Manor," though never a true manor house) is the oldest building in Jamaica. The kitchen in the rear is the original farmhouse, dating to 1730. In 1805 Rufus King, congressman and senator, and active in the Constitutional Convention, bought the property and about 1806 built the main part of the house, seen here. It was later the home of his son, John Alsop King, Governor of New York 1857 to 1858; the house was deeded to the Town of Jamaica in 1897 and since 1900 has been cared for by the King Manor Association. In 1986 a generous Federal grant made possible the complete refurbishing and restoration of the house. *(Photo by Charles Van Riper; Van Riper collection.)*

40. PETTIT'S HOTEL, 1905. Though now gone for over eighty years, Pettit's Hotel, on what is now Jamaica Avenue near Parsons Boulevard, was an authentic Jamaica landmark because George Washington really slept here in 1790, calling it in his diary "a pretty good and decent house." It was then known as the "Queen's Head" and had been well supported by the officers and men of the occupying British Army. It was here, on December 8, 1783, that Jamaica celebrated Evacuation Day, when the British troops marched out, by firing a volley and building a Liberty pole. In the nineteenth century the inn became a stagecoach terminal. The place went through

39

40

41

many hands, the best-known proprietor having been Alonzo B. Pettit, who ran the place from 1875 to 1896. The venerable old place was finally demolished in 1906. *(Photo by Frederick J. Weber; The Queens Borough Public Library.)*

41. FULTON STREET (JAMAICA AVENUE) FROM WEST OF FLUSHING AVENUE (PARSONS BOULEVARD), LOOKING EAST, ca. 1905. A fine general view of Jamaica about 1905, before the building of the elevated railroad along Jamaica Avenue (Fulton Street at that time). Jamaica was at this time in transition; a few modern buildings still standing today are visible at Herriman and Union Avenues (161st and 162nd Streets), but many old residences from the 1840's and 1850's still survived at the time of this photograph. The "el" came in 1917–18 and quickly commercialized Jamaica Avenue; within five years this stretch became the shopping and business center for all central Queens, with many fine stores, banks and theaters. *(Photo by Frederick J. Weber; The Queens Borough Public Library.)*

42. BEAVER POND, MARCH 1906. Beaver Pond, also known as Remsen's Pond (after its last owner, a Mr. Remsen), a natural pond in the heart of Jamaica, was one of the attractive features that induced the first settlers to select this spot for a village site in 1656. It lay just east of 150th Street, and Liberty Avenue today passes through the center of it. In the eighteenth century, horse races were run around it. This view of the pond, taken in March 1906, is the only one known and the last one as well; in June the pond was filled in and streets cut through. (*Brooklyn Daily Eagle photo, April 3, 1906.*)

43. BERGEN AVENUE (MERRICK BOULEVARD) FROM GROVE STREET (90th AVENUE), LOOKING NORTH, 1908. The most aristocratic section of Jamaica as it looked on a winter's day in 1908. All the houses on Hardenbrook, Clinton and Bergen Avenues (164th and 165th Streets and Merrick Boulevard) were big Victorian structures, almost mansions by our standards, boasting cupolas, turrets, towers, stained-glass stair windows and broad wraparound porches. Note the Peace Monument at the head of the street. All these fine proud homes have succumbed to the wrecker's ball, and apartment houses now loom in their place. (*Photo by Frederick J. Weber; The Queens Borough Public Library.*)

44. HILLSIDE AVENUE, LOOKING WEST, 1910. The Peace Monument in the middle of Hillside Avenue at Bergen Avenue (Merrick Boulevard). This bronze statue of Victory commemorating the fallen in the Civil War was dedicated on Memorial Day in 1896 and was paid for by public subscription from all over Queens. The artist was Fred W. Ruckstull (1853–1942), a prominent sculptor of heroic statues, an editor and the vice president of the Municipal Art Society. As traffic in Jamaica grew, the statue base was often sideswiped or rammed by cars, and, after a long campaign, the statue was relocated to the little park at 175th Street where it languishes unseen. The private house at the left is now a funeral home. (*Photo by Frederick J. Weber; The Queens Borough Public Library.*)

44

45. FLUSHING AVENUE (PARSONS BOULEVARD), 1914. A street that has changed incredibly. This peaceful scene shows Parsons Boulevard looking north from 89th Avenue (then Flushing and Shelton Avenues) in 1914. St. Mary's Church at the right was replaced by a modern structure in 1927. All the trees are gone, and the street is now the main artery leading to the Parsons Boulevard subway station, with throngs of people hurrying along the sidewalks, and cars and buses filling the roadway. *(Photo by Frederick J. Weber; The Queens Borough Public Library.)*

Jamaica 29

46. TOWN HALL, ca. 1915. The Town Hall of Jamaica, on the northeast corner of Jamaica Avenue and Parsons Boulevard, was built in 1870 at a cost of $70,000. Besides rooms for the various officials, it had a great hall, measuring 67 by 81 feet, on the second floor for Town meetings and social functions. After 1898, when Jamaica became a part of New York City, the old building was turned over to the Municipal Court, the Sheriff's office and the Traffic Court. It was torn down in 1941. *(Photo by Frederick J. Weber; The Queens Borough Public Library.)*

47. JAMAICA AVENUE AT 163rd STREET, 1921. A typical view of Jamaica for many years—Jamaica Avenue under the shadow of the "el." The photo looks west from 163rd Street, with rows of stores on both sides of the street. In 1977 the el was closed down, and in 1980 the structure was removed as far as Sutphin Boulevard, letting in the light. During 1986-87 Jamaica Avenue was completely repaved and recurbed, and brick sidewalks were installed, greatly enhancing the appearance of the street. (Photo by Frederick J. Weber; The Queens Borough Public Library.)

Jamaica 31

48. "EL" TERMINAL, 168th STREET AND
JAMAICA AVENUE, 1921. A circus parade
is just beginning. Note the aged wooden
stores and the private house on the corner;
Jamaica Avenue shrinks to only sixty feet
wide east of this corner. The avenue was
widened from here through Hillside, Hollis
and Bellaire during 1931–32, and, in the
1960's, 168th Street was widened at this corner and curved to fit its continuation north of
Jamaica Avenue. The el itself came down in
1980. *(Photo by Frederick J. Weber; The
Queens Borough Public Library.)*

Jamaica   33

49. JAMAICA AVENUE FROM UNION
HALL STREET, 1935. Where are all the
people and the cars? This is Jamaica Avenue
looking west from Union Hall Street on a
quiet Sunday morning in 1935. Burden's, a
long-established clothing store, is at the right,
and Plaut Bros. is advertising in its windows
its final liquidation sale; Woolworth's, on the
corner of 161st Street, really sold things for
nickels and dimes at that time. The banks and
trust companies were concentrated here, the
financial heart of Queens. *(Photo by Frederick J. Weber; The Queens Borough Public
Library.)*

50. JAMAICA AVENUE FROM MERRICK BOULEVARD, 1937. The "theater district," looking west. On the right is the legendary Valencia Theatre, which opened in 1931, one of the four Moorish-style cinema palaces in Queens. The more modest Alden Theatre is across the street. Ludwig Baumann's furniture building is on the corner, with the street floor leased to Wallach's, clothiers. *(Photo by Frederick J. Weber; The Queens Borough Public Library.)*

51. JAMAICA AVENUE AT 163rd STREET, LOOKING WEST, 1940. The Gertz department store, Goodwin's women's-and-infants'-wear store and the J. Kurtz furniture store are all readily identifiable here. *(Photo by Frederick J. Weber; The Queens Borough Public Library.)*

SPRINGFIELD

Springfield lies in the southeastern part of Queens and covers the general area on both sides of Merrick Boulevard and between New York Boulevard and the Nassau County line. The area is very old; the original rural village lay along Springfield Boulevard south of the Long Island Rail Road, where a few mid-eighteenth-century and early-nineteenth-century houses remain, in poor condition. Springfield Cemetery was established as early as 1670. Most of Springfield was farmland till World War I days, when development first began. Between 1920 and 1930 the population ballooned from 3,046 to 13,089, with many of the newcomers Brooklyn people in search of a suburban home. In 1927 the name of the entire community was changed to the more elegant "Springfield Gardens" (also the name of a housing development within Springfield, begun in 1906). Most of the community today is residential, with block on block of the two-and-a-half-story frame dwellings so typical of Queens neighborhoods.

---

52. TOMBSTONE, ca. 1900. The oldest surviving stone in the Springfield Cemetery, that of Jean Cornell, wife of William, who died in 1761. The child's face on top was the eighteenth-century way of representing the soul of the departed, which was now taking flight for heaven. Few brownstone memorials have survived; the vast majority of the stones in Springfield Cemetery are nineteenth- and twentieth-century marble and granite monuments. *(Photo by Charles Van Riper; Van Riper collection.)*

53. L. E. DECKER'S GENERAL STORE, NORTHWEST CORNER OF SPRINGFIELD AVENUE (NOW BOULEVARD) AND MERRICK ROAD (BOULEVARD), APRIL 14, 1904. The occasion for the picture was the running of the first Long Island road race via Merrick Road from Jamaica to Babylon and return on April 14; the auto is chain-driven and has exactly one cylinder! *(Suffolk County Historical Society collection.)*

54. HENRY FURTHOFER'S SPRINGFIELD HOTEL, SOUTHEAST CORNER OF SPRINGFIELD AVENUE AND MERRICK ROAD, April 14, 1904. Another participant in the April 14 auto race is seen here. In those days a beer manufacturer would give a hotel proprietor a big wire advertising sign featuring his name and that of his hotel in prominent gold letters if, in return, he would agree to handle their brand exclusively. *(Suffolk County Historical Society collection.)*

52

54

55

55. BAYLIS' POND, ca. 1905. Children skating on Nostrand's or Baylis' Pond, now a city-owned lot on the southeast corner of 219th Street and 141st Avenue. Springfield Brook alongside Springfield Boulevard was a flowing stream down to the 1920's, fed by the runoff from the fields on either side. At intervals the stream was dammed up to form millponds, with one at Merrick Road (Nostrand or Baylis') and one at 147th Avenue (Higbie's or Cornell's). The Higbie family operated a saw- and gristmill at the pond outlet at 147th Avenue through much of the nineteenth century. *(From a postcard; The Queens Borough Public Library.)*

56. OLD HOUSE NEAR 147th AVENUE, 1905. A house of colonial vintage back of the millpond near what is now 147th Avenue as it looked in 1905. The kitchen wing at the left is probably the original seventeenth- or eighteenth-century house, with a later early-nineteenth-century addition. Other early features are the "six-on-six" windows downstairs and the "eyebrow" windows at the front. *(From a postcard; Vincent F. Seyfried collection.)*

57

57. HARBOR HAVEN, ca. 1910. This 1910 development of recreational cottages was located on the south side of the Rockaway Turnpike, 1,335 feet south of Springfield Avenue (or Road). In the rear can be seen a vast stretch of marsh and meadowland, through which ran serpentine creeks and occasional canals. Access was almost exclusively by the trolley running from Jamaica to Far Rockaway; here a fourteen-bench open car of 1902 vintage has stopped to let off a vacationer. Note the swimming pool in the lower left corner. *(From a postcard; The Queens Borough Public Library.)*

38 *Springfield*

58. SPRINGFIELD AVENUE LOOKING NORTH FROM THE RAILROAD STATION, MARCH 14, 1910. The station is just out of view to the right. The Presbyterian church across the tracks dates from 1865. The pillars and arbors at the left call attention to the newly promoted "Springfield Gardens," launched in 1906. Only farmhouses and farm wagons are in view in this eighty-year-old photo. (*L.I.R.R. photo; Robert Presbrey collection.*)

59. SPRINGFIELD AVENUE FROM 137th AVENUE, LOOKING SOUTH, MARCH 14, 1910. Springfield station is at the left. The tower on the Peter Nostrand house at 186-19 140th Avenue can be barely glimpsed in the middle distance, to the left of the railroad-crossing sign and behind the pillars advertising the new Springfield Gardens. Old Public School 161 is visible to the right of the pillars. (*L.I.R.R. photo; Robert Presbrey collection.*)

60. MERRICK ROAD (BOULEVARD), LOOKING EAST FROM 180th STREET, MARCH 20, 1914. The Merrick Road makes a reverse curve here as it approaches Springfield, the houses of which can be seen at the right. Vast tracts of empty land appear at the left, and most of the visible dwellings are farmhouses. (*L.I.R.R. photo; Robert Presbrey collection.*)

61. FIRST METHODIST EPISCOPAL CHURCH OF SPRINGFIELD, FARMERS AVENUE (BOULEVARD) AND DENNIS AVENUE, 1916. Still standing, this church was established here in 1867. The parsonage stands at the left. Note the early automobile with acetylene lamps mounted on the hood. *(Photo by Frederick J. Weber; The Queens Borough Public Library.)*

62. SAMUEL HIGBIE HOUSE, NORTH-EAST CORNER OF SPRINGFIELD BOU-LEVARD AND 141st ROAD, JANUARY 18, 1959. The Higbie house dates back to about 1770. Families like the Higbies, Baylises, Hendricksons and Nostrands all had farm-houses here during the Revolution, and British soldiers forced the owners to provide fire-wood and foodstuffs to support the occu-pation between 1776 and 1783. This house is still standing. *(Photo by Vincent F. Seyfried.)*

62

LONG ISLAND CITY

Long Island City, as a whole, is the largest community in Queens in both area and population. It embraces five neighborhoods: Astoria, north of Broadway; Hunter's Point, south of Broadway to Newtown Creek; Ravenswood, along the waterfront; Steinway, on either side of the important street of that name; and Dutch Kills, in the Queens Plaza area. Each of these is distinctive with respect to land use and architecture. Hunter's Point contains the railroad yards and most of the factories and light-industry plants, plus the new fifty-story Citicorp tower. Ravenswood has its big housing project and waterfront public-utility buildings. Astoria and Steinway are residential, with block on block of two- and six-family houses, interspersed with the massive Mathews flats and many surviving single-family dwellings. Long Island City was the first community to become multiethnic; in 1900 it was heavily Irish, German, Czech and Italian, and today Astoria is home to the largest Greek colony in America. To experience the flavor of Long Island City one has only to tour the three main shopping streets: 30th Avenue, Steinway Street and Broadway. The motion-picture complex at 35th Street and 35th Avenue, including the Astoria Studio and the American Museum of the Moving Image, is another "must."

63. OLD QUEENS COUNTY COURT HOUSE, ca. 1895. The old Queens County Court House was built in 1874 to serve all Queens County (then including Nassau County). In 1904 a tinsmith repairing the roof set fire to the cupola and the whole roof fell in. Five years of rebuilding resulted in the present Court House, which was opened in 1909 and is almost double the size of the 1874 structure. (*Photo by Paul Geipel; Queens Historical Society collection.*)

64. L.I.R.R. FERRY TERMINAL, ca. 1905.
The 34th Street ferry terminal at the foot of
Borden Avenue is seen here (behind the
trolleys) in its glory days, about 1905. Two
lines of ferries, the Long Island Rail Road and
eight trolley lines all came together here,
making this corner the busiest on all Long
Island. On big holidays like the Fourth of July
and Labor Day, as many as ten thousand
people streamed here from New York, pushing and elbowing their way onto the trains
and trolleys. *(From a postcard; The Queens
Borough Public Library.)*

64

65. QUEENSBORO BRIDGE PLAZA, 1911.
Looking west toward the Queensboro Bridge.
An elaborate staircase at the end of the plaza
gave access to the two footpaths on the
bridge. In the foreground is a flower-bed
crescent and sunburst, with other plantings
visible in the two other squares. When the
elevated came in 1914, all these plantings and
open spaces disappeared. *(Photo by N.Y.C.
Bureau of Plants and Structures; N.Y.C.
Municipal Archives.)*

66. QUEENSBORO BRIDGE PLAZA, 1912.
Looking east from the Queensboro Bridge. In
the foreground is the 161-foot-high mast from
Sir Thomas Lipton's yacht *Shamrock III*. Put
up in November 1909, it was taken down in
August 1914 because of the elevated-station
construction. *(Photo by N.Y.C. Bureau of
Plants and Structures; N.Y.C. Municipal
Archives.)*

67. QUEENS BOULEVARD AT VAN DAM STREET, LOOKING EAST, APRIL 29, 1913. This is one of the most crowded spots in Long Island City today. The Packard Building on the southeast corner still stands. Beyond the two new buildings in the picture, there is mostly emptiness as far as the eye can see; the three automobiles parked in front of the Packard factory are the only sign of life. The sign over the awning on the one-story building (center) reads "John D. Engelken's Cafe." *(Photo by N.Y.C. Board of Transportation; Robert Presbrey collection.)*

68. THOMSON AVENUE AT JACKSON AVENUE, LOOKING WEST, 1915. The courthouse building is at the left and St. John's Hospital at the right. The street is still unpaved, with no curbs. It will be a year before the Court House Square station on the elevated opens (February 15, 1916). There are almost no cars and no people. The hospital site is now (1990) that of the new Citicorp tower. The courthouse building still stands, now housing a branch of the New York State Supreme Court. *(Photo by Frederick J. Weber; The Queens Borough Public Library.)*

69

68

69. ELEVATED LINE, QUEENBORO PLAZA, ca. 1917. This station is familiar to everyone using the number 7 and "N" lines (originally part of the IRT and BMT systems, respectively) in north Queens. When this station was erected in 1915–16, it was the most complicated elevated station in the country, accommodating four different lines on two levels. The 2nd Avenue el ceased operating to this point in 1942. In the 1950's, train operation was simplified by running what is now the number 7 line to Flushing alone and the present "N" line to Astoria alone. The whole north side of the station was then torn down. *(N.Y.C. Municipal Archives.)*

Long Island City   **47**

72

73

70. VIEW FROM PACKARD BUILDING, JANUARY 12, 1917 (LOOKING WEST). Looking west along Queens Boulevard from the roof of the Packard Building. Some tracks have yet to be laid on the elevated line. The vast Sunnyside Yards of the Pennsylvania Railroad lie ahead and in the distance are Queensboro Bridge Plaza and the huge Brewster Building. Note the empty lots in the foreground, all below street grade. *(Photo by N.Y.C. Board of Transportation; Robert Presbrey collection.)*

71. VIEW FROM PACKARD BUILDING, JANUARY 12, 1917 (LOOKING EAST). Looking east along Queens Boulevard from the roof of the Packard Building. The gleaming new elevated structure is just about finished but not yet opened. (The station is 33rd Street.) Queens Boulevard in the foreground is a two-lane road with a trolley track on either side. All of Sunnyside lies open and undeveloped all the way out to Woodside in the distance; within ten short years the whole area would be built up. *(Photo by N.Y.C. Board of Transportation; Robert Presbrey collection.)*

72. "MATHEWS MODEL FLATS," 1917. This remarkable ad shows a whole long block of "Mathews Model Flats" on 13th Avenue (48th Street) near Jackson Avenue (Northern Boulevard) completed in 1917. The Mathews firm specialized in these attached six-family apartment houses, done in buff and brown decorative brick, topped with a bracketed cornice and entered by stone stoops with cast-iron railings. Mathews was especially active in Ridgewood, Astoria and Woodside. *(From an advertising brochure.)*

73. ST. JOHN'S HOSPITAL, ca. 1918. For years a landmark in Long Island City, at Jackson and Thomson Avenues, opposite the Court House, St. John's opened in January 1899. It was then the only large modern hospital in Queens; within a very short time, new wings had to be built on either side to accommodate the heavy demands on its facilities. On its site is being built the fifty-story Citicorp tower, the highest building on Long Island. *(From a postcard; Vincent F. Seyfried collection.)*

74. **L.I.R.R. FERRY TERMINAL, 1922.** The foot of Borden Avenue at 2nd Street, Long Island City, in 1922, is a ghost street here but was the busiest on Long Island (see photo 64, above) before the Queensboro Bridge opened. Miller's Hotel, a famous political hangout in Mayor Gleason's day, was converted to a warehouse in 1915. The 34th Street ferry was shut down three years after this photo was taken, in 1925. The old main depot of the Long Island Rail Road, standing at the left, lost all its traffic in 1910, when the railroad tunnel to Pennsylvania Station in Manhattan was opened. *(Photo by Eugene Armbruster; N.Y.C. Municipal Archives.)*

11-10-31

e 2

n Blvd N W Cor 50TH Ave (4TH St

75. TROLLEY LOOP, NOVEMBER 10, 1931. The busy corner of Vernon Boulevard and 50th Avenue. The police station at the left is still standing today; the trolley loop for the Brooklyn cars has been converted into a parking lot. All the old buildings on Vernon Boulevard are still standing; St. Mary's church is just out of sight to the right. *(Photo by N.Y.C. Board of Transportation; Robert Presbrey collection.)*

76. HACKETT BUILDING, MAY 19, 1935. The first Borough Hall (1898–1916), the Hackett Building, at 10-63 Jackson Avenue, corner of 49th Avenue, on May 19, 1935. All the borough offices were installed in 1898 in this building, a former dress-fabric store built in the 1870's. As the business of Queens expanded, the building became less and less adequate, until in 1916 the city took over a new building in Queensboro Bridge Plaza. St. Mary's Church is at the right. *(Queens Topographical Bureau.)*

77. LONG ISLAND CITY DOCKS, SEPTEMBER 16, 1937. Activity along the docks. The skyscrapers of Manhattan may be seen through the masts of the ships. *(Photo by John Drennan; Nassau County Museum Reference Library).*

78. "CARFLOATS" ON THE EAST RIVER AT LONG ISLAND CITY, FEBRUARY 3, 1945. *(The Queens Borough Public Library.)*

ASTORIA

Astoria owes its existence to Stephen Alling Halsey, who incorporated the village in 1839; it was named after John Jacob Astor, pioneer in the fur trade with the Pacific Northwest. Centered on the waterfront at first, Astoria expanded inland in the 1870's as developers bought up farms and laid out streets. The Steinways came in 1870 and founded Steinway Village around their waterfront piano factory. The coming of rapid transit and the five-cent fare triggered a boom in housing in the 1920's, at first mostly in private houses and six-family apartment houses, and later in multistory buildings. Astoria today is the largest residential section in Long Island City and one of the most sought-after areas by apartment hunters.

79. ST. GEORGE'S CHURCH RECTORY, ca. 1905. The oldest surviving building in Astoria—the parsonage of St. George's Episcopal Church at Franklin and Woolsey Streets (27th Avenue and 14th Street). Built in 1840 to serve as a private girls' academy in the new village of Astoria, it failed to attract funding and instead became a parish hall. Originally facing Woolsey (14th) Street, it was moved to this site in 1903 to make room for the new St. George's Church. (*Long Island Savings Bank collection.*)

80. THE "HILL," 1906. Twelfth Street and 14th Street north of 27th Avenue were the aristocratic streets of old Astoria, the "Hill" where the best people lived in the best houses. This view looks up 14th Street (then Woolsey Street) from 27th Avenue (then Franklin Street) in 1906; most of the houses still stand, but the one at the right was demolished in 1987 for a row of apartments. (*From a postcard; Vincent F. Seyfried collection.*)

81. SCHUETZEN PARK, ca. 1908. Schuetzen Park, between Steinway Avenue and Albert Street (now Steinway and 41st Streets) south of Broadway, was the most famous outdoor garden and picnic park in Astoria from the time it opened in 1870 till it closed in 1924. The trees all have whitewashed trunks in this view; picnic tables can be seen in the foreground and a dancing pavilion at the right. When this picture was taken, a lot of Astoria in the background was still open land. (*Geipel collection, Queens Historical Society.*)

82. SECOND AVENUE (31st STREET) AT GRAND AVENUE (30th AVENUE), LOOKING NORTH, MARCH 21, 1913. A busy place today, totally changed. The Astoria "el" runs on this street now, and the station darkens the street below. *(Robert Presbrey collection.)*

83. ASTORIA SQUARE, ca. 1915. Astoria Square, formed by Main, Willow and Franklin Streets (Main Avenue, 18th Street and 27th Avenue), was and is the nearest thing to a village center in Astoria. The flatiron-style building in the middle, still standing, was for years Gally's furniture store; on the left is Main Street, now Main Avenue, with a trolley car carrying passengers from the 92nd Street ferry; one of New York's "white wings" sweeps the street in front. On the right is Franklin Street, now 27th Avenue, once lined with fine houses. *(From a postcard; Vincent F. Seyfried collection.)*

83

84. STEINWAY AVENUE (STREET) FROM ASTORIA BOULEVARD, LOOKING NORTH, 1915. Everything in the picture has disappeared except the massive New York Connecting Railroad bridge. The little Arena Theatre, with its limited seating capacity of 150, was a victim of the big movie palaces of the '20's, and the saloon was put out of business by Prohibition. Astoria Boulevard was widened in 1934 for the Grand Central Parkway. *(Photo by Frederick J. Weber; The Queens Borough Public Library.)*

Astoria   57

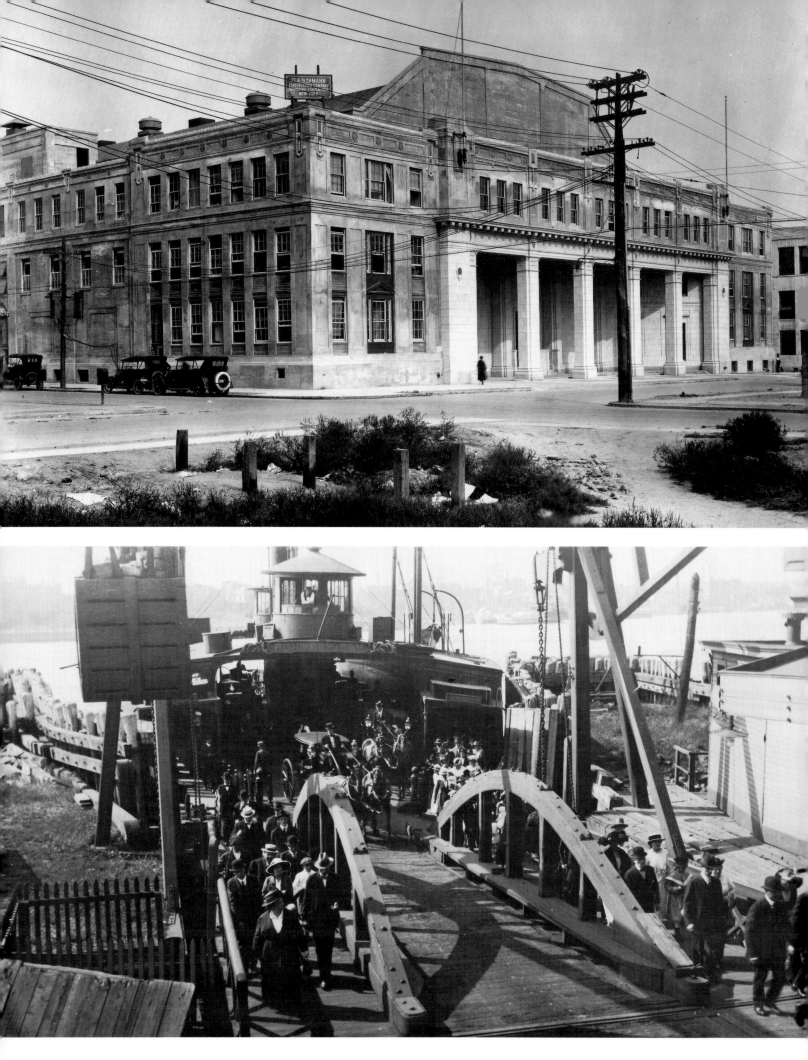

85. ASTORIA STUDIO, SEPTEMBER 1920. The front of the Astoria movie-studio building on 35th Avenue at 35th Street as it neared completion in September 1920. Built by Famous Players–Lasky Corporation (Paramount Pictures after 1927) in a sparsely inhabited part of Long Island City bordering Astoria, this huge building covers an entire square block. Though its four front columns and huge vaulted roof suggest a railroad terminal, its numerous windows and cavernous interior made it ideal for movie making. The building's location near the heart of New York, the financial and cultural capital of the country, and its closeness to rapid transit and to bridges, tunnels and major arteries combined to make it the great rival of the Hollywood studios. Still active today as Kaufman Astoria Studios (the largest film studio in the East), this facility has been used for the production of virtually every kind of film, from full-length features—some of them star-studded classics—to Army training films to commercials. *(From the collection of The American Museum of the Moving Image, Astoria, N.Y.)*

86. FERRY TERMINAL, FOOT OF ASTORIA BOULEVARD, 1921. The 92nd Street ferry terminal when the city was operating it; the *Bowery Bay* is unloading its cargo of passengers. The city shut down the ferry operation on August 1, 1936, when the Triborough Bridge opened. *(Collection of La Guardia Community College, Long Island City, N.Y.)*

87. REAL-ESTATE AD, JUNE 10, 1923. Astoria's Ditmars section was developing rapidly when this ad was run. These attractive, low-cost houses were modern in design, affordable and within two or three blocks of the Astoria "el" with its five-cent fare. All are still standing today and have appreciated ten times over in value. *(From the* New York Herald.*)*

NORWOOD GARDENS, L. I.
RICKERT-BROWN REALTY CO.
52 VANDERBILT AVE., N. Y.

89

88. 30th AVENUE FROM 27th STREET, LOOKING EAST, ca. 1925. One of Astoria's busiest shopping streets, still called Grand Avenue on this old postcard. The apartments and stores on either side have changed little over the years and the "el" still runs on 31st Street. The street was then macadamized but not yet blacktopped. *(From a postcard; Vincent F. Seyfried collection.)*

89. NORWOOD GARDENS, MID-1920'S. Norwood Gardens, along 35th, 36th and 37th Street between Broadway and 30th Avenue, was one of the most attractive private-home developments erected in the mid-1920's. These houses were put up by the Rickert-Finlay Co. of Flushing and each featured quality construction, a luxury interior, eight rooms, two baths and a garage. Prices ranged from $9,000 to $15,000. *(From an old brochure.)*

90. BROADWAY FROM STEINWAY STREET, LOOKING WEST, ca. 1927. The Bank of the Manhattan Company at the left was opened in 1926; in the distance can be glimpsed the Astoria "el" on 31st Street. The trolley tracks have been gone since 1939, and most of the buildings have had their fronts modernized since this picture was taken about 1927. *(From a postcard; Vincent F. Seyfried collection.)*

91. BAR INTERIOR, 1934. A typical Astoria bar on 18th Street and 27th Avenue in 1934. The tin ceiling and fixtures survive from pre-Prohibition days, but the portrait of Franklin D. Roosevelt, the cathedral radio and the stock are new. *(Photo by Henry Dehls; Robert F. Eisen collection.)*

QUEENS VILLAGE

Queens Village in colonial times was known as the Little Plains, and much of it was "commons," publicly owned land for grazing cattle. In the eighteenth century a few roads were laid out and farms established. In 1824 Thomas Brush established a blacksmith shop, prospered, built shops and a factory, and the settlement began to be called Brushville in recognition of his enterprise. By vote of the inhabitants the name was changed to Queens in 1856. Development began in 1870 and 1871 south of Jericho Turnpike. Additional subdivisions were marketed between 1906 and 1915. The big housing boom struck Queens in the '20's when row houses by the hundreds sprang up on newly opened streets north of Jericho Turnpike and south of Hollis Avenue. To avoid confusion between the village and county names, the Long Island Rail Road in 1923 changed the station name to Queens Village, and so it has remained. Today Queens Village is a mature community, wholly residential, and retains its suburban character and appearance.

92. JUNCTION OF JERICHO AND HEMPSTEAD TURNPIKES (JAMAICA AND HEMPSTEAD AVENUES) AT 212th STREET, LOOKING EAST, ca. 1910. The three-story building at the left is all in this picture that survives today. Fox's East End Hotel on the other corner died with Prohibition, and the Rose farmhouse, almost completely obscured by trees, succumbed in the 1920's. Thomas Callister's wagon works, founded in 1853, was the biggest industry in Queens Village, turning out farm wagons for all the local farmers. In later years Callister went in for automobiles and built a modern showroom in 1926. *(Photo by Frederick J. Weber; The Queens Borough Public Library.)*

93. CREED AVENUE (SPRINGFIELD BOULEVARD), LOOKING NORTH TO JERICHO TURNPIKE FROM THE LONG ISLAND RAIL ROAD CROSSING, SEPTEMBER 6, 1911. A scene that has changed incredibly. All the houses at the left were torn down in 1923 to create a large open station plaza. All the buildings at the right were torn down in 1927 to build a big Loew's theater with stores and offices facing on Springfield Boulevard. The Reformed church is barely visible in the middle distance. *(L.I.R.R. photo; Robert Presbrey collection.)*

94. JACKSON AVENUE (220th STREET), ca. 1915. Typical housing of the 1910–18 era in Queens Village—large houses with full attics and cellars, and each one architecturally distinct from its neighbors on 40-by-100-foot lots. In the 1920's houses became smaller, more uniform and more crowded. *(From a postcard; Vincent F. Seyfried collection.)*

95. JUNCTION OF SPRINGFIELD ROAD (BOULEVARD) AND HOLLIS AVENUE, 1915. Public School 34 is at the left. The site was chosen in 1897 and the building erected in 1898 but politics delayed the opening until June 4, 1900; in later years, the building had to be enlarged. Note the farmer's barn at the extreme left. St. Joachim and Anne's Catholic parish was founded in 1897 and the church built in 1898 on former farmland. The church grew enormously in the 1920's and '30's, and in 1968 a new, very modern edifice was built. *(Photo by Frederick J. Weber; The Queens Borough Public Library.)*

96. SPRINGFIELD BOULEVARD, 1920's. A scene typical of the 1920's—new home owners with the kids and the family "flivver." This was the great era of tract housing, block after block of Dutch Colonials, all on 25-by-100-foot city lots, and all retailing for an affordable price, usually $7,000 to $12,000. *(From a postcard; Vincent F. Seyfried collection.)*

97. HEMPSTEAD AVENUE AT SPRINGFIELD BOULEVARD, LOOKING WEST, JULY 30, 1933. One of the best-known corners in Queens Village. The street has just been widened and the trolleys have just four months more to run. All of the stores and most of the houses are still standing but the period-piece diner has long vanished. *(Photo by Frederick J. Weber; The Queens Borough Public Library.)*

98. COMMUNITY THEATER, AUGUST 1934. The little Community theater was Queens Village's first movie house; the cornerstone had been laid on February 22, 1924. For a long time the building served not only as a theater but also as a meeting hall for civic and fraternal organizations, something that Queens Village had long lacked. In 1927–28 the Loew's chain built a big modern theater, but the little Community hung on till the 1960's. *(From a postcard; Vincent F. Seyfried collection.)*

Queens Village   65

WOODSIDE

Woodside got its name from John A. F. Kelly, part owner of a Brooklyn newspaper, whose father had moved to the Woodside area in 1826. He used to send to his paper for publication chatty little dispatches from his rural home, entitled "Letters from Woodside." When Benjamin Hitchcock bought into the Kelly farm for a development, he adopted the name Woodside for his proposed village. In 1867 he filed his plan and began selling lots at $100 each. A railroad station was established at 58th Street and 38th Avenue. Hitchcock's success attracted other developers, and a small village grew up; the 1890's witnessed the doubing of the population, which reached 3,878 in 1900. The arrival of the trolley in 1895 and the elevated in 1917 greatly stimulated the growth of the village. Although Woodside is still primarily a community of one-family houses, light industry occupies a few blocks along the western border, and apartment houses have gained a foothold on the eastern edge. Many Hispanics have been attracted to Woodside since World War II, principally Colombians, Ecuadorians and Dominicans; Asians constitute about ten percent of the population.

99. PLAN OF FIRST HOUSING DEVELOPMENT, DECEMBER 1867. The original development plan filed by Hitchcock for Woodside in December 1867, covering the area from Woodside Avenue to 61st Street. There are 972 numbered lots indicated on the plan. John A. F. Kelly, the original owner, has retained the frontage on Woodside Avenue from Third to Seventh Streets (56th to 60th Streets) for himself. Models for four styles of house, from mansion to cottage, decorate the blank spaces, plus a view of the original railroad station at Seventh (60th) Street. (*The Queens Borough Public Library.*)

100. WOODSIDE STATION, WINTER, 1871–72. The oldest known Woodside photograph. This incredible view shows what was to become 58th Street and the old Woodside railroad station at 38th Avenue during the winter of 1871–72. The village is less than five years old, only a handful of houses have gone up and the woods stretch out as far as the eye can see. The engine *New York* of the Flushing and Woodside Rail Road is pulling three matchbox coaches past a sign reading "Look out for the cars." A. P. Riker's real-estate office is at the right. (*The Queens Borough Public Library.*)

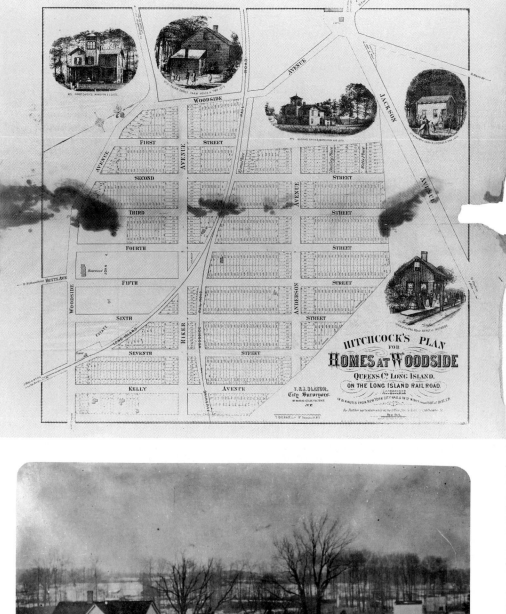

101. KELLY AVENUE (61st STREET) FROM WOODSIDE AVENUE, LOOKING NORTH, ca. 1905. It is hard to recognize in this picture one of the busiest corners in "downtown Woodside." All the private houses have now vanished; a bank now occupies the corner at the right. Roosevelt Avenue has been cut through a block down the street and the elevated line and Long Island Rail Road are now in sight. *(From a postcard; Vincent F. Seyfried collection.)*

Woodside 67

102. L.I.R.R. AND ELEVATED STA-TIONS, 1920. A scene that has changed little in seventy years—the intersection of the elevated line with the Long Island Rail Road at 61st Street in 1920. The el began running in 1917; the railroad had been relocated and lowered at this point in 1915. The little apartment house at the left was built in 1916, the first in Woodside. The big Victorian houses glimpsed under the el on 61st Street have yielded to commercial structures. *(Photo by Frederick J. Weber; The Queens Borough Public Library.)*

103. STREETCAR BARNS, 1929. The former Woodside car barns of the New York & Queens County Railway as they looked in 1929. When these barns were built in 1896, Woodside Avenue at the right marked the city limits of Long Island City, and Woodside was the "country." All the trolleys from Flushing, College Point, Jamaica and Long Island City were serviced here, and passengers changed cars for the different routes. *(Photo by N.Y.C. Board of Transportation; Robert Presbrey collection.)*

104. STREETCAR BARNS, APRIL 1987. The same barns today. After the trolleys departed in 1939, the barns became the headquarters for trucking and express companies. In 1986, Ciampa Bros. of Flushing bought this big site; they are currently developing it into a shopping mall. The corner towers and former waiting room will remain as historic reminders of an earlier day. *(Photo by Sunnyside Redevelopment Corp.)*

105. BROADWAY AT ROOSEVELT AVENUE, LOOKING NORTH, OCTOBER 6, 1932. The last important street opening in Woodside—the cutting of the tape and throwing open to traffic of Broadway from Roosevelt Avenue to Woodside Avenue. Ten months later, on August 19, 1933, the Independent Subway opened to this corner, making it an important traffic junction. A passenger-transfer connection between the el and the subway now occupies the space at the right. *(Photo by N.Y.C. Dept. of Highways; The Queens Borough Public Library.)*

ROCKAWAY

Rockaway in colonial times was an uninhabited wasteland of sand and scrub growth, but, as early as 1833, a seaside hotel was built in Far Rockaway that lasted till 1864. The South Side Railroad extended down the peninsula in 1869, bringing the first excursionists; the Long Island Rail Road followed in 1872, and its cross-bay line arrived in 1880. Hotels, boarding houses, saloons, amusement houses and baths sprang up by the dozen over the next thirty years. Everyone could afford Rockaway—the round-trip fare by rail was only fifty cents and the beach shared with Coney Island the status of being New York's favorite summer resort. Rockaway as a group of residential communities was slower to develop; Rockaway Beach in 1890, Arverne in 1887, Belle Harbor and Neponsit in 1908. By World War I the city had acquired the waterfront and built sections of boardwalk. Michael P. Holland, Luke Eldert and Louis C. Hammel built resorts named after them; William Wainwright built Playland and Seaside to provide popular amusement. The opening of the Cross Bay Bridge and the Marine Parkway effectively made Rockaway a part of Queens and the greater city.

106. WAINWRIGHT'S BEACH, 1906. The good old days at Rockaway Beach eighty-five years ago—Wainwright's bathing beach between Beach 102nd and 103rd Streets on a weekend in 1906 when thousands of people thronged the shore to escape the heat of the tenements. Rockaway, like Coney Island, was a poor man's playground, with four miles of beautiful white sand accessible for as little as ten cents via the Brooklyn elevated lines. *(From a postcard; The Queens Borough Public Library.)*

107. STATION OF U.S. LIFE SAVING SERVICE, 1911. Rare photo of the interior of a lifesaving station at Arverne in 1911. The whole south coast of Long Island had stations such as this at intervals of a few miles, ready to come to the rescue of coastward vessels in distress. The longboat at the left is filled with gear at the ready and coils of rope lie close to hand. The men are reading books just dropped off by the traveling library. (*The Queens Borough Public Library.*)

108. ROCHE'S BEACH, ca. 1922. Roche's Beach at Far Rockaway was very different from the crowded resorts at Rockaway Beach, with their amusements, boardwalks, noise and crowds. This was a family beach catering to women and children, and the bathhouses in the background offered only saltwater taffy and a pail-and-shovel for the children. The trolley from Far Rockaway station terminated right in the bathhouse; Beach 19th Street is just to the right of the large cottage. (*The Queens Borough Public Library.*)

109. OCEAN PROMENADE FROM 73rd STREET, LOOKING WEST, MAY 25, 1939. Within a very few years flooding and salt spray killed off the white pines and carefully seeded grass in the foreground. More recently, in the last ten years Rockaway has battled an unusual erosion problem, with sections of boardwalk undermined by winter storms. (*The Queens Borough Public Library.*)

110. CENTRAL ROCKAWAY, MAY 28, 1939. Aerial view of Rockaway peninsula from about Beach 84th Street on the right to about Beach 103rd Street on the left. Cross Bay Boulevard runs through Broad Channel in the center and enters Rockaway Beach between Beach 94th and 95th Streets. The Long Island Rail Road cross-bay trestle, which was to burn out in 1950, has a much straighter alignment. Idlewild (later Kennedy) International Airport has not yet taken over the entire marshlands and water area in the upper right with its runways and terminals. (*The Queens Borough Public Library.*)

111. PLAYLAND, ROCKAWAY BEACH, 1945. The Playland amusement complex in 1945, with the ocean promenade and Beach 98th Street in the foreground. The bulb terminus of Cross Bay Boulevard appears at the top, along with the concrete viaduct of the Long Island Rail Road running from west to east. Playland was the last surviving large amusement park in Rockaway; when skyrocketing insurance premiums forced its closure in 1987, it marked the end of an era. (*Rockaway Chamber of Commerce and The Queens Borough Public Library.*)

112. WALKWAY, PLAYLAND, AUGUST 3, 1956. This photo of a typical Rockaway summer crowd is a study in social change. Many of the men are wearing suits and ties, and all the women are neatly turned out in dresses and suits. The era of slacks, jeans, rock-and-roll outfits, jumpsuits, pantsuits, etc., is still a few years in the future. (*Rockaway Chamber of Commerce and The Queens Borough Public Library.*)

Rockaway   77

DOUGLASTON

Douglaston is one of the smallest areas in Queens, occupying a narrow peninsula above Little Neck. Its situation, facing Little Neck Bay on three sides, enables many of the property owners to enjoy water views; in addition, the village is well wooded with mature trees, not only along the winding, scenic Shore Drive but also on almost every front lawn. Douglaston is named after William P. Douglas, a Scotsman who in 1835 bought the peninsula from Wynant Van Zandt, whose splendid 1819 mansion is now the Douglaston Club. In 1906, the Rickert-Finlay Company began the development of Douglaston, laying out streets and erecting beautiful, spacious homes. Douglaston today is still wholly residential and ranks as one of the most exclusive and affluent areas in Queens County.

113. DOUGLAS MANOR (MAP), 1906. The Rickert-Finlay map of 1906, showing 57 blocks, each divided into anywhere from forty to eighty 20-by-100-foot lots. Home owners were required to buy at least three such city lots before building. The north-south streets were curved to avoid a city grid pattern and to provide pleasing sight ines. Development was slow at first but boomed in the 1920's. (Vincent F. Seyfried collection.)

114. VAN VLIET HOUSE, 1908. This old house, about a block north of the railroad station, was used as Public School 98 for many years, serving the needs of Douglaston to as late as 1931, when the successor school was built on the same site. The medieval tower is a pleasing example of Victorian whimsy. (N.Y.C. Board of Education photo; Vincent F. Seyfried collection.)

115. DOUGLAS MANOR, ca. 1910. Types of houses erected by the Rickert-Finlay developers between 1906 and World War I; many were large, like the one in the foreground, and required servants to maintain. All the windows have summer awnings, an amenity almost extinct in our day, and the roof is Spanish tile, a touch of luxury. Most Douglaston plots have 80- or 100-foot fronts, allowing for big houses and generous landscaping. (From a postcard; Vincent F. Seyfried collection.)

113

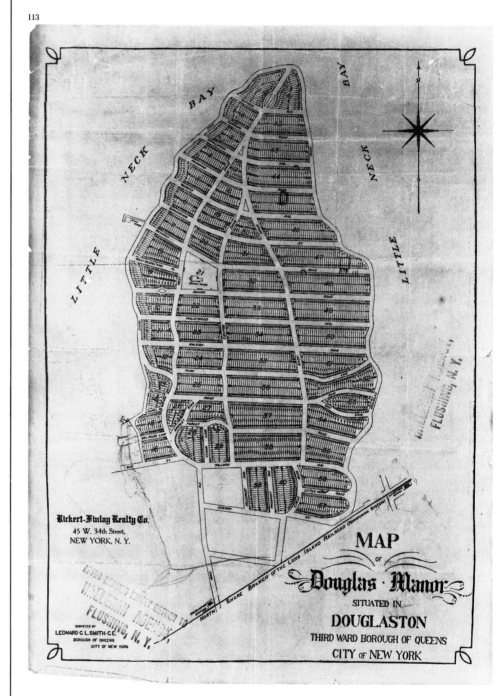

Rickert-Finlay Realty Co.
45 W. 34th Street,
NEW YORK, N. Y.

SURVEYED BY
LEONARD C. L. SMITH C.E.
BOROUGH OF QUEENS
CITY OF NEW YORK

MAP
OF
Douglas · Manor
SITUATED IN
DOUGLASTON
THIRD WARD BOROUGH OF QUEENS
CITY OF NEW YORK

Residences in Douglas Manor, L. I.

116

118

119

116. DOUGLAS MANOR INN, ca. 1910. The historic manor house at Douglaston, built by Wynant Van Zandt in 1819 and now the home of the Douglaston Club. It was bought by William P. Douglas, the father of Douglaston, who lived in it for years. In 1906 the venerable building was sold to the Douglas Manor Association and in 1921 to the Douglaston Club. The house is set off by majestic trees, and its rooms are very large and admirably adapted for club use. *(From a postcard; Vincent F. Seyfried collection.)*

117. MAIN AVENUE (DOUGLASTON PARKWAY), AT L.I.R.R. CROSSING LOOKING NORTH, OCTOBER 13, 1910. At left is old Public School 98, supplanted by a modern structure today. Note the advertising sign at the extreme left offering land by the acre. Today all the open land and all the wooded area in the picture has been built on. Douglaston station is just out of sight to the right. *(L.I.R.R. photo; Robert Presbrey collection.)*

118. L.I.R.R. STATION, OCTOBER 13, 1910. The first Douglaston depot opened in May 1867 and was named in honor of the community founder, William P. Douglas. In April 1887 Douglas and some of his wealthy friends contributed $6,000 to build this Queen Anne–style depot, which served Douglaston until March 1962. *(L.I.R.R. photo; Robert Presbrey collection.)*

119. ZION CHURCHYARD MONUMENT, ca. 1936. A picturesque stone monument in Zion churchyard: "Here rest the last of the Matinecocks." The Matinecock Indians once occupied the whole North Shore from Flushing east to Cold Spring Harbor, embracing both Little and Great Neck. A small Indian burial ground used to face Northern Boulevard. When that thoroughfare was widened in 1931, the bones were taken up and reinterred in Zion churchyard. On November 1, 1931, this Indian plot was dedicated with appropriate ceremonies. The great rock, split in two to the ground, is the distinctive symbol of the Matinecocks, and the tree growing between the two halves stands as a living memorial to an ancient people. *(The Queens Borough Public Library.)*

PEYTONA AND FASHION.
IN THEIR GREAT MATCH FOR $20,000.
OVER THE UNION COURSE L. I. MAY 13TH 1845, WON BY PEYTONA
Time 7: 39¾ 7: 45¼.

PEYTONA red Chestnut, Rider, Blue jacket Black cap.   FASHION light Chestnut, Rider, Purple jacket, Green cap.

121

WOODHAVEN

Woodhaven lies in the southwest part of Queens along the Brooklyn border, extending from 76th Street to 100th Street and from Forest Park to Rockaway Boulevard. John R. Pitkin, a Connecticut Yankee, founded the village in 1835, but the establishment of a tinware factory in 1863 by two Frenchmen, Messrs. Lalance and Grosjean, really launched Woodhaven as a residential and manufacturing community. The breakup of the neighboring farms in the 1880's and '90's provided room for rapid development. Streets were cut through and long rows of attached brick and wooden houses were erected, the characteristic housing pattern here. Since private autos were not foreseen, alleyways and garages were not provided. By 1914, Woodhaven was almost fully built up. The community today is stable, very well maintained and still wholly residential. Woodhaven Boulevard, Jamaica Avenue and Atlantic Avenue are the principal thoroughfares, while Forest Park provides a playground for the village.

120. UNION COURSE, MAY 13, 1845. The Union Course racetrack was one of the most famous in the country; it opened in 1821, and Southern plantation owners brought up their best horses to race against Northern challengers. This scene looks west from what is now 84th Street to the grandstand at 78th Street. At left is the Long Island Rail Road station, and, at the far right, Jamaica Avenue and the hills that later became Cypress Hills Cemetery. The Union Course was broken up in 1888 and the land sold for housing. *(From a chromolithograph; Vincent F. Seyfried collection.)*

121. THE "WYCKOFF," 1895. A landmark building, the Wyckoff, at 93-02 95th Avenue. Built in 1889 as the home of the Woodhaven Real Estate Exchange, it became the Woodhaven Bank. It is still standing today, but its fine Moorish cupola and Victorian balustrade have vanished. *(The Queens Borough Public Library.)*

122

Entrance to Dexter Park, Union Course, L. I.

123

122. DEXTER PARK ON THE BROOKLYN AND JAMAICA PLANK ROAD (JAMAICA AVENUE), OPPOSITE THE HEAD OF DREW AVENUE (75th STREET), ca. 1905. On this fondly remembered site a roadhouse was built in 1851 to accommodate the racing crowds at Union Course. It was managed by Hiram Woodruff, the most famous horse trainer and racer of his day. The park was named after the racehorse Dexter, who ran heats here in the 1850's and was later buried on the grounds. Besides the hotel seen here, later managers added dancing pavilions, a carousel, bowling alleys and a baseball park. The baseball field and bleachers continued in use till the mid-1950's, when most of the site was sold for apartments. *(From a postcard; Vincent F. Seyfried collection.)*

123. OCEAN VIEW AVENUE (89th STREET), FROM 300 FEET NORTH OF JAMAICA AVENUE, 1908. Typical Woodhaven housing: two-story brick attached residences with tin bracketed cornices over decorative swag designs. There are no alleyways between the houses, for private autos have not yet become affordable. Note the rutted, unpaved street. *(From a postcard; Vincent F. Seyfried collection.)*

124. FOREST PARKWAY, ca. 1912. The show street of Woodhaven: Forest Parkway as it looked about 1912. This, the only 80-foot-wide residential street in Woodhaven, marked the center of the Forest Parkway development of 1900. Though only six blocks long, Forest Parkway was macadamized from the start, and big homes on 40-foot-minimum lots were built to line its length. Many of these survive today as doctors' and dentists' offices; a few are still private residences. *(From a postcard; Vincent F. Seyfried collection.)*

Woodhaven   85

Ferry St., Woodhaven, L. I.

125. FERRY STREET (86th STREET) FROM JAMAICA AVENUE, LOOKING SOUTH, ca. 1914. The scene is almost unchanged today. The café is still on the corner but without its fancy glass-canopied entrance, and all the houses along 86th Street are still standing. *(From a postcard; The Queens Borough Public Library.)*

126. LALANCE AND GROSJEAN PLANT, ca. 1940. The huge three-story building extended from 91st to 95th Street along the south side of Atlantic Avenue. Started in 1863, the firm grew, becoming the largest kitchenware plant in the country, with 2,000 workers and spreading over 1,100 acres. The company shut down in 1955, and in 1984 most of the factory was razed for a neighborhood shopping center. The corner with the clock tower, however, was saved and converted into the Columbia Federal Savings Bank, which has rehabilitated the century-old brick tower and set the clock going once again. *(Photo by Frederick J. Weber; The Queens Borough Public Library.)*

127. JAMAICA AVENUE AT 100th STREET, LOOKING EAST, 1947. Brooklyn Manor railroad station is at the right; the railroad service was abandoned in 1962. The Jamaica Avenue elevated line, overhead, was opened in 1917. The trolley stopped running in 1947 and was replaced by buses. *(L.I.R.R. photo; Robert Presbrey collection.)*

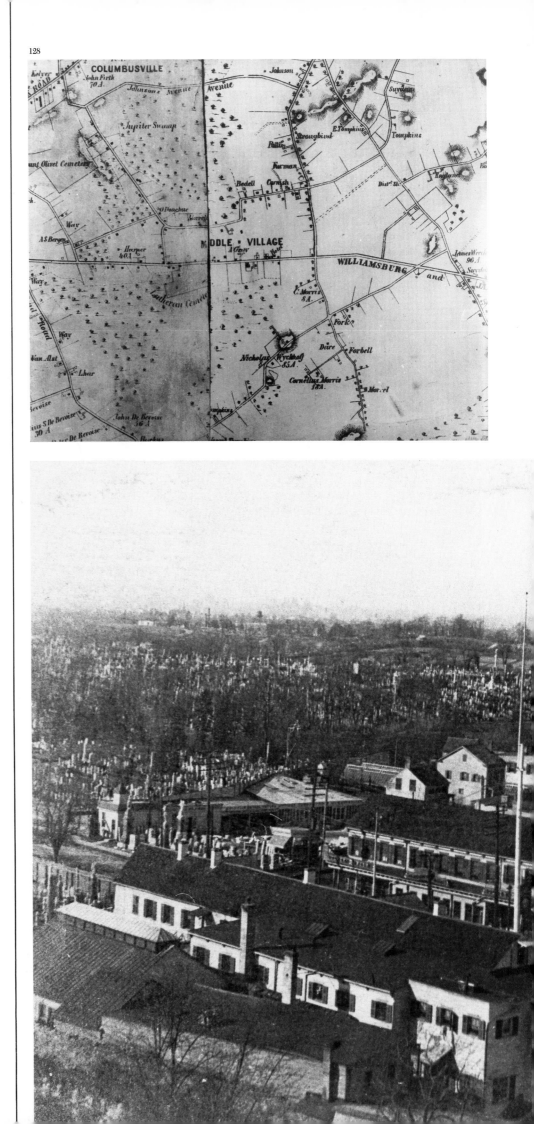

MIDDLE VILLAGE

Middle Village grew up about 1830 and received its name because it marked the midpoint for farmers on the long wagon haul between the Brooklyn ferries at the foot of Broadway, and Jamaica. Metropolitan Avenue was laid out in 1814 and completed in 1816 as a turnpike road with toll gates at each end. Middle Village for years was a typical one-street town with small scattered houses strung out along the Williamsburgh and Jamaica Turnpike (now Metropolitan Avenue) between Fresh Pond Road and Dry Harbor Road. Just before and after the Civil War, a three-story brick hotel at what is now 75-43 Metropolitan Avenue was the rendezvous for farmers, offering a night's lodging and refreshments. North of the village lay the primeval and impenetrable Juniper Swamp; part of it is now Juniper Valley Park.

The coming of the cemeteries to Middle Village changed its character; Lutheran south came in 1852, Lutheran north about 1860 and St. John's in 1879. Nurseries, saloons and hotels grew up in profusion to meet the demands of cemetery visitors. In the 1920's the housing boom struck the village; streets were laid out on either side of Metropolitan Avenue, Dry Harbor Road and Cooper Avenue, and in short order row upon row of houses stretched out to join those of Glendale and Maspeth and Forest Hills on the borders. Middle Village was an Anglo-Saxon community down to the Civil War; for a century it remained heavily German; in modern times Yugoslavs and Italians have moved in in substantial numbers.

128. MIDDLE VILLAGE, 1852. The Williamsburgh and Jamaica Turnpike is now Metropolitan Avenue and the north–south road is now Dry Harbor Road; what became 69th Street is at the left, and Juniper Valley Road and Furmanville Road border on Juniper Swamp (on this old map "Jupiter Swamp"). *(Detail, Dripps Map.)*

129. OLD MIDDLE VILLAGE, ca. 1900. In the foreground is Niederstein's Hotel and across the street J. N. F. Sieb's Hotel, now a garage; at the right is John Sutter's monument works. Old Trinity Lutheran Church is on 69th Street. The Lutheran Cemetery in the background still has a lot of empty space; Maspeth can be glimpsed on the horizon. *(From a postcard; The Queens Borough Public Library.)*

130. TRINITY LUTHERAN CHURCH, ca. 1907. This building was erected on the brow of a hill in Lutheran Cemetery in 1907 to replace the little wooden building on Juniper Avenue (69th Street). The church was struck by lightning on May 21, 1975, and its interior burned out. A new church was erected on Dry Harbor Road and Juniper Boulevard South. *(From a postcard; Vincent F. Seyfried collection.)*

Middle Village   89

131

131. METROPOLITAN AVENUE FROM DRY HARBOR ROAD, LOOKING WEST, ca. 1910. On the left is the St. John's Hotel of John Braun, now a marble yard, and on the right is Peter Becker's Columbia Park Hotel, now Ottavino's monument works. The carriage shed still stands. The trolleys stopped running in June 1949 and many of the old wooden buildings have disappeared. (Robert F. Eisen collection.)

132. NIEDERSTEIN'S RESTAURANT, INTERIOR, 1910. Note the ice chest, the trophies on the wall from Niederstein's Adirondack hunting expeditions and the "air conditioning"—fans connected by leather belting to a motor in the rear. Bentwood chairs and checkered tablecloths were hallmarks of the era. (Niederstein collection and Vincent F. Seyfried collection.)

133. FEARLESS HOOK & LADDER COMPANY NO. 7, 71-55 METROPOLITAN AVENUE, ca. 1913. Organized in 1891, this volunteer company protected the village until displaced by the city's Fire Department in September 1913. The building survived for years as a store until its demolition on August 15, 1986. (Photo by Frederick J. Weber; The Queens Borough Public Library.)

134. HISTORIC NIEDERSTEIN'S HOTEL, METROPOLITAN AVENUE AT 69th STREET, ca. 1939. Built by Henry Schumacher about 1865, it became John Niederstein's hotel in 1888. Niederstein had been a cook in Germany, came to America in 1866 and in the '80's operated the Yorkville Assembly Rooms at 1393 2nd Avenue, New York. He gave his Middle Village place the name "Grand Hotel" and enlarged it by adding wings on either side. There were 32 rooms available on the second floor. For years, funeral parties constituted the bulk of the business, but wedding parties, banquets and family dinners were an important source of income. Memorial Day was the biggest holiday of the year, closely followed by Mother's Day and June 5 (Slocum Memorial Day, commemorating the tragic sinking and burning of the boat General Slocum in the East River on that day in 1904). In the 1970's the hotel was modernized by new owners, who removed the old-time porch and carriage sheds. (The Queens Borough Public Library.)

134

CORONA

*C*orona began in the classic manner of Queens communities: a group of developers bought nine farms and laid them out in streets and building lots (1854). The same year, the National (later Fashion) Race Course attracted national attention to Corona by locating here. Spotty development marked the 1870's and '80's, but the years from 1890 to 1918 witnessed housing construction on a large scale. By 1920 there was almost no empty land and the '20's were a period of infilling and the beginnings of apartment building. The opening of the elevated railroad along Roosevelt Avenue to 104th Street in 1917 transformed Corona from a semirural village to a densely settled community.

Corona down to 1950 was the home of mostly Germans, Irish, Swedes and English, with a large concentration of Italians; after 1960 the black population reached twenty percent, but Hispanics from the Caribbean and South America now predominate.

135

137

138

135. FASHION COURSE, MAY 23, 1866. The Fashion Course, after the Union Course in Woodhaven, was the most famous race-track in early racing history; its location was between what is now 97th and 105th Streets and 34th and 37th Avenues in Corona. The track opened in 1854 with speed racing and later turned to trotting races; it went out of business in 1872 and a few years later was cut up into streets and building lots. *(From a chromolithograph; Vincent F. Seyfried collection.)*

136. FASHION COURSE, ca. 1860. Grandstand of the Fashion Course, built somewhat like a medieval fortification. Carriages and stagecoaches from New York and Brooklyn parked in front, while saloons and hotels catered to the passengers. The track's best years were from 1854 to 1861, when the outbreak of the Civil War put an end to all North–South sports competition. *(From an old woodcut; Vincent F. Seyfried collection.)*

137. COE HOUSE, HORSE BROOK NEAR COLONIAL AVENUE, ca. 1900. This house, if it were standing today, would be the oldest in Queens County. The Robert Coe house, built about 1655, was erected on the west side of Colonial Avenue at a point now in the middle of the Long Island Expressway. Across the street was once a millpond and gristmill to grind corn and wheat, which provided the livelihood for a succession of occupants of the old house. Both the house and Horse Brook were destroyed in 1930 to lay out Horace Harding Boulevard, now the Long Island Expressway. *(From a 1905 calendar; The Queens Borough Public Library.)*

138. MILESTONE, JACKSON AVENUE (NORTHERN BOULEVARD), ca. 1900. Northern Boulevard, earlier Jackson Avenue and originally the road of the Hunter's Point, Newtown and Flushing Turnpike Company, was incorporated on April 16, 1857, and opened for business on July 13, 1860. From the beginning people called the road Jackson Avenue after John C. Jackson, who had planned the road and guided it to completion. It was the only road in Queens County to be adorned with milestones. Three were still standing in 1916; the last survivor was taken up in November 1987 at the urging of the Queens Historical Society and is on exhibition at the Langston Hughes Library in Corona. *(Photo by Charles Van Riper; Van Riper collection.)*

94   *Corona*

139. SCHOOLYARD, P.S. 92, ca. 1908. Playing baseball near Jackson Avenue (Northern Boulevard), corner of 100th Street, on the sandlot behind Public School 92 about 1908. The 1893 building on the corner is still standing but the trees and the cupola-topped mansion in the rear are gone. (*From a postcard; Vincent F. Seyfried collection.*)

140. GRAND AVENUE (ROOSEVELT AVENUE) AT SYCAMORE AVENUE (104th STREET), AUGUST 1908. A scene almost impossible to identify without a little help. The street in the foreground is Grand Avenue (Roosevelt Avenue) and the camera looks up Sycamore Avenue (104th Street). Today the elevated runs along Roosevelt Avenue, the 104th Street station occupies the corner, and Corona Square takes up all the space at the bottom of the photograph. Corona in 1908, like many other places in Queens, was a rural village made up of private houses and plenty of empty spaces, but the coming of rapid transit and the five-cent fare urbanized the whole area. (*From a postcard; Vincent F. Seyfried collection.*)

141A. PUBLIC SCHOOL 10, 1908. Exterior view of Public School 10, the "Frog Hollow" or Bowery Bay school on the southwest corner of Astoria Boulevard and 90th Street. It was the last one-room schoolhouse in Queens and lasted until 1930. The tiny school accommodated 26–29 students at most. (*N.Y.C. Board of Education photo.*)

141B. PUBLIC SCHOOL 10, JUNE 1910. An interior view of the only room in the Bowery Bay school. (*Brooklyn Daily Eagle photo.*)

142. CORONA SCHOOLROOM, NOVEMBER 1910. Everyone is dressed up in his Sunday best on this great occasion of a formal classroom portrait. Note the precise Palmer-method handwriting of the teacher on the board and the inspirational message for the day heading the lesson. Corona had five elementary schools and the largest pupil enrollment in the Second Ward (old Newtown). (*The Queens Borough Public Library.*)

143. UNION EVANGELICAL CHURCH
OF CORONA, ca. 1910. The oldest surviving
building in Corona, the Union Church on
National Street at 42nd Avenue. The first
service was held on June 5, 1870, and the
church continues in use to this day. Some of
the ornamental ironwork and gingerbread
decoration have succumbed to time, and the
woods around and behind the church have
disappeared, but the structure is still solid.
National Street is a dirt road here in this 1910-
era photo. (From a postcard; Vincent F.
Seyfried collection.)

143

144. PUBLIC SCHOOL 16 ACROSS LIN-
DEN LAKE FROM 103rd STREET, LOOK-
ING EAST, ca. 1930. In colonial days the
farmers of Corona watered their cattle here in
this natural pond. As the village grew up all
around Linden Lake, it saw use as an ice-
skating rink in winter and as the backdrop for
band concerts in summer. Years later, the
pond became choked with mud and silt and
the Parks Department filled it in in 1947. In
this 1930's photo a fountain throws up iri-
descent spray over a shimmering surface.
(N.Y.C. Board of Education photo.)

Overleaf: 145–148. FLUSHING MEAD-
OWS, LOOKING SOUTH, NOVEMBER 9,
1935. This remarkable panoramic photo (divided here into four parts) shows the vast
expanse of Flushing Meadows as it appeared
before it was radically altered for the 1939
World's Fair. The bridge at the right (photo
148) remains today. The bridge in photo 147,
carrying Corona Avenue across the Flushing
River, was once informally known as "Paddy
Mara's Bridge," after the man who tended it.
Along the route of Horace Harding Boulevard the Long Island Expressway runs
through the site of this photograph today.
(Photo by Queens Topographical Bureau;
The Queens Borough Public Library.)

Corona Ave.

Flushing River

Horace Harding Blvd.

149. NEW YORK WORLD'S FAIR, AERIAL VIEW, LOOKING WEST, 1939. Dominating this photo—and the entire fair—are the 700-foot-high Trylon and 200-foot-wide Perisphere at the heart of the fair's Theme Center. Surrounding them are various buildings housing exhibits of government, business, industry and the arts. The neighborhood of Corona, just beyond the fairgrounds, has now, in the 31 years since the August 1908 photo above (see photo 140), assumed a totally different, far more urban character. (*The Queens Borough Public Library.*)

150. LOUIS ARMSTRONG HOUSE, 34-56 107th STREET, OCTOBER 1989. This modest house was for 28 years (1943-71) the residence of jazz legend Louis ("Satchmo") Armstrong. His wife Lucille continued to occupy it until her death in 1983, when it passed into the hands of the city and the care of Queens College. It is also a National Historic Landmark. The house as seen here evidences considerable alteration (much of it very recent) since its construction by builder Thomas Daly in 1910. (*Photo by Vincent F. Seyfried.*)

COLLEGE POINT

College Point on Flushing Bay, two miles north of Flushing, was founded by Conrad Poppenhusen in 1854 as a site for his works for making objects out of hard rubber, the plastic of the nineteenth century. Poppenhusen employed hundreds of workers to manufacture combs, brushes, dental and medical goods and hardware. The early village above 14th Avenue contained the palatial homes of the wealthy, while company houses and modest private houses filled the streets to the south and east. What is now College Point Boulevard was and still is the main business thoroughfare. Between the 1880's and World War I, College Point became renowned for its breweries and its many resorts catering to one-day-excursion parties. Point View Island, Freygang's, Zehden's and Donnelly's became as well known as North Beach. In World War I aircraft manufacture became established at the LWF Engineering Company plant. Since 1920, light industry has become increasingly important, especially on the streets near the waterfront. Now, condominiums are encroaching on the residential streets, attracted by the water views available on all sides.

---

151. BAR, JOSEPH WITZEL'S HOTEL, NORTHWEST CORNER OF SECOND AVENUE AND NORTH 10th STREET (NOW 14th ROAD AND 119th STREET), ca. 1895. A typical prewar College Point saloon photographed some time in the 1890's. Amazingly, this barroom with its ornately carved wooden bar can still be seen in Flessel's Restaurant, the successor to Witzel's. (*Robert C. Friedrich collection.*)

152. VEGETABLE-DELIVERY WAGON, HIGH AND NORTH 14th STREETS (NOW 14th AVENUE AND 123rd STREET), ca. 1897. The neighborhood vegetable man— Anton Beresheim with his delivery wagon proclaiming "Fancy Fruit in Season." He carries a portable basket displaying a selection of fruits and vegetables for door-to-door sale. (*Photo by Jacob F. Wieners, Jr.; Robert C. Friedrich collection.*)

153. TYLER'S BATHING BEACH, FOOT OF FIRST (NOW 14th) AVENUE ON THE EAST RIVER, ca. 1898. As usual, most of the ladies are observers rather than participants. Informal beaches like this were common along the shores of Flushing Bay and Long Island Sound. In 1916 the Board of Health shut down commercial bathhouses because of increasing pollution, but tolerated bathing by those who wore suits under their clothes. By the mid-1920's swimming in inland Queens waters had disappeared altogether. *(Robert C. Friedrich collection.)*

154. SLEDDING ON FIRST AVENUE AT NORTH 11th STREET (NOW 14th AVENUE AT 120th STREET), WINTER, 1901. The still-standing Reformed Church can be glimpsed through the trees at the right. There isn't much of a hill on the street but the boys are making the most of it. Bobsleds holding eight or ten riders were popular in this era. *(Robert C. Friedrich collection.)*

155. GEORGE HACHTEL'S BAKERY, SECOND AVENUE AT 6th STREET (NOW 115-17 14th ROAD), ca. 1905. Mr. Hachtel poses proudly in front of his bakery with his elegantly lettered delivery wagon, flanked by his driver, his apprentice boy, his employees and members of his family. *(Robert C. Friedrich collection.)*

College Point 105

156. DINING HALL, CHARLES J. FREY-GANG'S PAVILION, ca. 1910. The biggest industry in College Point in the days before Prohibition was catering to excursion parties that came by boat and trolley to the beer gardens, saloons, hotels and dance halls for a day's outing. Many were political clubs from Manhattan and Brooklyn. Note the heavy crockery and the bentwood chairs typical of the period. *(Robert C. Friedrich collection.)*

157. BLACKSMITH AT WORK, NORTH 14th STREET (NOW 123rd STREET) BEHIND ST. FIDELIS' ROMAN CATHO-LIC CHURCH, ca. 1910. A truly rare scene—a blacksmith shoeing a customer's horse. Valentine Krapp is servicing one of his waiting customer's two horses in front of his College Point shop. Note the big horseshoe sign advertising the shop on the pole at the left. *(Robert C. Friedrich collection.)*

158. BUTCHER-SHOP INTERIOR, ca. 1910. Rare inside view of a College Point butcher shop about 1910. A sign "Merry Christmas" hangs overhead, and wreaths and garlands decorate the ceiling. Hanging in the rear are slabs of beef along with chickens with their wing feathers left unplucked. Signs on the counter proclaim meat for sale at twelve and sixteen cents per pound. *(Photo by Jacob F. Wieners, Jr.; Robert C. Friedrich collection.)*

159. MILKMAN'S SLEIGH, FIRST (NOW 14th) AVENUE, ca. 1910. Borden's Dairy delivering milk by sleigh in the good old days. The driver is heavily dressed with boots and gloves, and sits on his horse's folded woolen blanket. Twelve milk bottles fill the wooden milk boxes piled up three deep behind the driver. Note the lantern in front of the sleigh for early-morning delivery. *(Photo by Jacob F. Wieners, Jr.; Robert C. Friedrich collection.)*

160. LWF COMPANY AIRCRAFT PLANT, 1918. This company was organized in 1915 by Messrs. Lowe, Willard and Fowler, whence the name; in 1916 they began making a two-passenger training biplane, the Model "F," designed to be equipped with various engines. This factory was one of the first in the United States constructed specifically for the manufacture of aircraft. The LWF company dissolved in 1924. *(Photo by Jacob F. Wieners, Jr.; The Queens Borough Public Library.)*

John C. Debevoise

RIDGEWOOD

The Ridgewood area was in colonial times part of the Wyckoff and Debevoise farms, which were gradually broken up over a period of a hundred years. When the street-railway companies built carbarns in the 1860's and '80's on land that was then just over the Brooklyn line in Queens County, their workmen and car crews began settling the new hamlet of Ridgewood. When the Myrtle Avenue "el" reached Ridgewood in 1889, the village grew rapidly. Most of the housing was built from 1900 to 1920, particularly by mass builders like Paul Stier and Gustave Mathews. Ridgewood has always been heavily German, conservative, frugal and middle-class, although in recent years Yugoslavs, Puerto Ricans and blacks have moved into the southern and western fringes. Myrtle Avenue is the principal business street, with many stores and banks; the population has stayed roughly at about 60,000. The old-time breweries have all disappeared, but small knitting mills continue the tradition of local industry. In 1986 Ridgewood was declared a historic district, and the Onderdonk House keeps alive the area's Dutch beginnings.

161. JOHN C. DEBEVOISE AND HIS HOUSE, 1882. The still-standing John C. Debevoise house on the southwest corner of Fresh Pond Road and Catalpa Avenue (originally Myrtle Street), built about 1848. Debevoise was born in 1815 and died childless in 1897, leaving 24 acres lying roughly between Catalpa and 70th Avenues, Myrtle Avenue and Fresh Pond Road. The old house is now considerably altered from what it was in this 1882 engraving; it has recently served as a senior citizens' center. (*Robert F. Eisen collection.*)

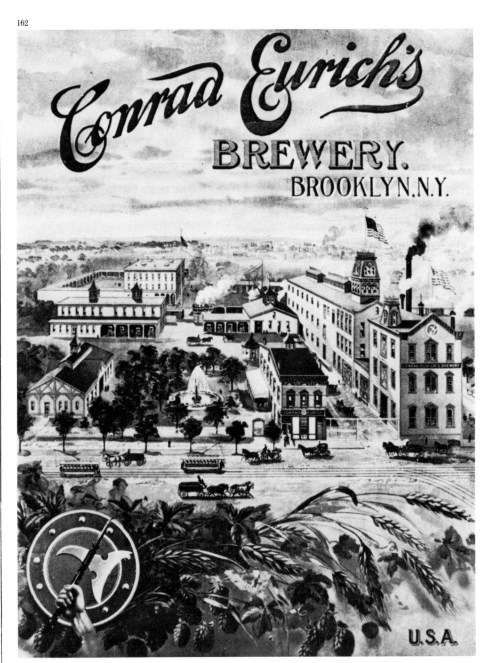

162. EURICH BREWERY, 1900. Conrad Eurich's Brewery on the south side of Wyckoff Avenue at Halsey Street as it appeared on a calendar put out by the company in 1900. This brewery passed through several changes of ownership and as many names: Leibinger & Oehm (1887–1895), Conrad Eurich (1899–1903) and, finally, the Elm Brewing Company, which went out of business in 1907. All the proprietors used the hand-and-axe symbol. The Brooklyn border is just back of the buildings. *(The Queens Borough Public Library.)*

163. VANDER ENDE-BEADEL-ONDER-DONK HOUSE, 1820 FLUSHING AVENUE, ca. 1900. On the Brooklyn-Queens border, this is one of the oldest houses in Queens County, the stone part dating back to about 1709, with traces of the older frame house going back to 1655. Vandals badly damaged the house by arson in February 1975 but the Greater Ridgewood Historical Society has restored the building, fenced the grounds and made it into a living museum of Queens's Dutch heritage. *(From a postcard; Vincent F. Seyfried collection.)*

164. WELZ & ZERWECK BREWERY, ca. 1905. For several decades up until about seventy years ago, Ridgewood was an important brewing center. Within a radius of about five blocks there were five big operators: the Welz & Zerweck Brewery, the Frank Brewing Company, the Elm (Eurich) Brewing Company, the Diogenes Brewing Company and the George Grauer Brewery. Most went out of business in 1920 when Prohibition came in. In this promotional picture the Welz & Zerweck Brewery somewhat exaggerated the size of its plant, as did the Eurich Brewery in illustration 162. *(Robert F. Eisen collection.)*

165

165. ARBITRATION ROCK, ca. 1910. This massive boulder of dark, rough, irregularly shaped stone, situated at what was to become the junction of Onderdonk and Montrose Avenues, formerly marked the boundary between Queens and Brooklyn. The line here was the occasion for a hundred-year dispute lasting from 1660 to 1769, which created intense bitterness and extensive litigation. The rock was visible for years but was covered or destroyed when Onderdonk Avenue was extended west of Flushing Avenue in the 1930's. (*Queens Topographical Bureau collection.*)

166. PAINT-STORE INTERIOR, ca. 1910. Interior of the Platz Brothers painters'-supplies store, northeast corner of Gates and Forest Avenues. This store is still in business today, run as a hardware store by a descendant of one of the original Platz brothers. Note the transition in lighting: kerosene lamps side by side with electric lamps; a goose-neck telephone is at the right. The price of paint ranges from 45 to 75 cents a can. (*Robert F. Eisen collection.*)

167. GROCERY INTERIOR, 1912. Henry Lindemann's grocery and delicatessen at the southwest corner of 68th Avenue (originally Hughes Street) and Fresh Pond Road. Note the fresh flowers hanging from the ceiling; a large block of ice cools the delicatessen showcase. The store featured Adolf Gobel's meats. A coffee-grinding mill is at left. Fresh Pond Road is still a lively shopping center. (*Robert F. Eisen collection.*)

168. CIRCUS PARADE ON CYPRESS AVENUE, 1912. A Barnum & Bailey circus parade passes Kreuscher's Hotel, at the corner of Myrtle and Cypress Avenues. Kreuscher's opened in 1860 as Andrew Beck's Hotel on what had been the Nicholas Wyckoff farm. George Stroebel bought the place in 1871, and, at his death in 1878, John Kreuscher, his son-in-law, took it over. Aaron Levine ran movies at the right beginning in 1911; his was the first moving-picture theater in Ridgewood. Later Kreuscher's became a Labor Lyceum and, in the 1920's, a night club and speakeasy. *(Robert F. Eisen collection.)*

170

169. FRESH POND ROAD ELEVATED STATION, 1912. The tracks still ran on the ground at this point. The extension of the Myrtle Avenue "el" into Ridgewood in October 1906 is credited by real-estate developers as the primary reason for Ridgewood's runaway growth over the next two decades. *(Photo by N.Y.C. Board of Transportation; Robert Presbrey collection.)*

170. "MATHEWS MODEL FLATS," 1914. Gustave Mathews and his sons began building these solid, carefully crafted brick houses in Ridgewood in 1904. An apartment consisted of five rooms and bath, with an air shaft to give light to the interior bedrooms, all for rent at eighteen to twenty dollars a month. By 1917 over eight hundred of these "flats" had been built, mostly in Ridgewood but also in Astoria and Woodside. Pictured here are 1612–1674 Putnam Avenue under construction. *(The Queens Borough Public Library.)*

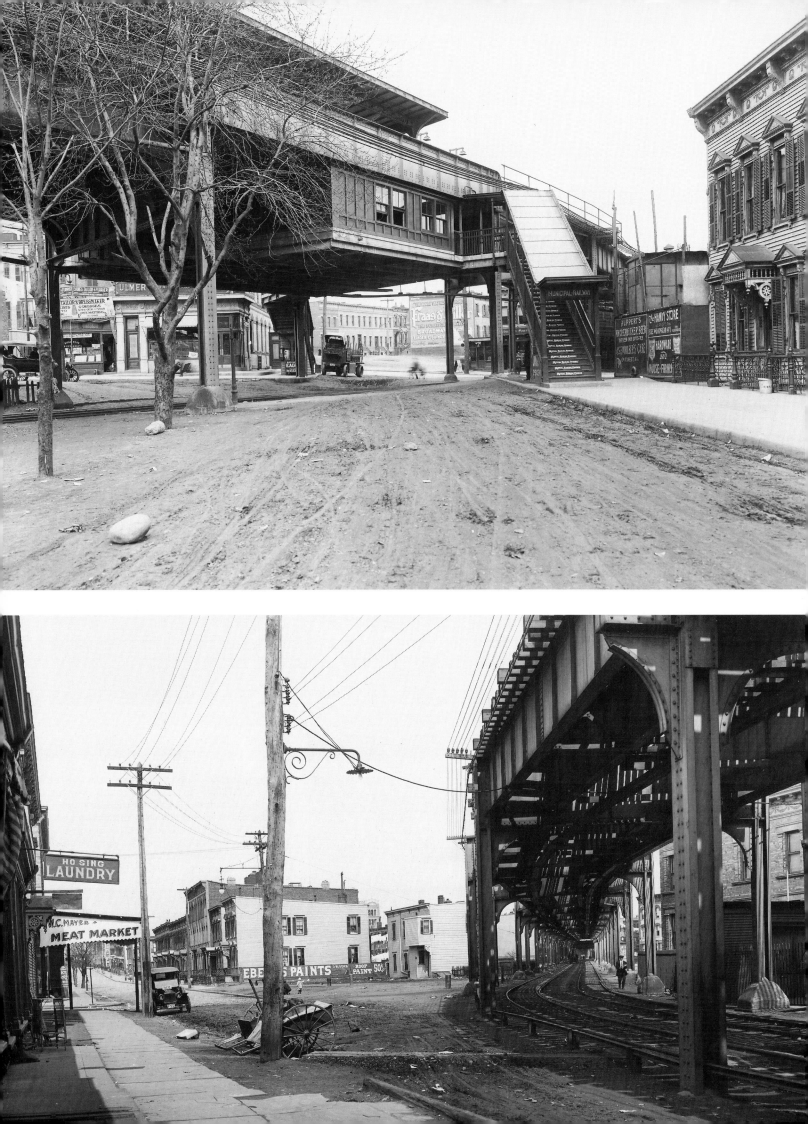

171

173

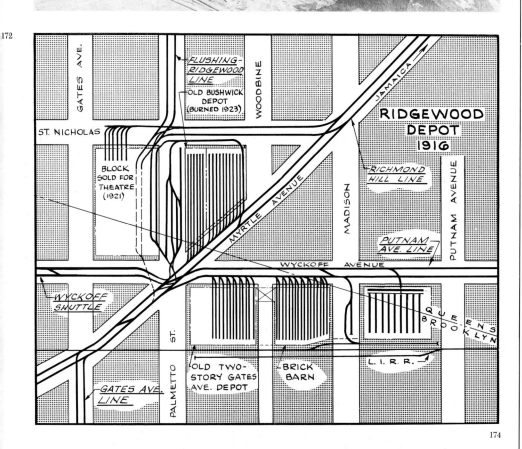

172

174

171. ELEVATED STATION, FOREST AVENUE, APRIL 28, 1916. This view looks up Putnam Avenue to Forest Avenue. Fairview Avenue is at the left; the houses in the middle distance are on a continuation of Putnam Avenue. The houses on the right show the elegant roof cornices with their brackets, wreaths and swags, the fine moldings on the windows and the ornate doorways once so common all through Ridgewood and Brooklyn. *(Photo by N.Y.C. Board of Transportation; Robert Presbrey collection.)*

172. LOOKING UP PALMETTO STREET TOWARD ONDERDONK AVENUE, APRIL 28, 1916. The "el" right-of-way, which turns off at this point, began as a steam railroad to the Lutheran Cemetery in 1881 and became a trolley line in 1895 and then a rapid-transit line running on the ground in 1906; the present elevated structure dates to February 1915. The fine architectural detail on the houses in the rear has in all too many cases disappeared under asphalt tile and aluminum siding. *(Photo by N.Y.C. Board of Transportation; Robert Presbrey collection.)*

173. BROOKLYN CITY RAILROAD DEPOT, AUGUST 29, 1916. This brick depot at Wyckoff and Myrtle Avenues was built in 1881 for the Gates Avenue and Myrtle Avenue trolleys. This car barn, plus the Bushwick railroad depot of 1860 across the street and, later, the Coney Island & Brooklyn Railroad car barn, created a huge street-railway complex that employed a great many men and was the direct cause of the first large-scale settlement of Ridgewood. Wyckoff Avenue was the border of the City (later Borough) of Brooklyn and the County (later Borough) of Queens. *(Photo by N.Y.C. Board of Transportation; Robert Presbrey collection.)*

174. MAP OF RIDGEWOOD DEPOT, 1916. Ridgewood depot was at its peak at this time, with about seventy storage tracks for streetcars, and tracks in just about every street, plus the Long Island Rail Road's Manhattan Beach Division. Today's Myrtle Avenue "el" riders making the turn at Myrtle Avenue and Palmetto Street would never suspect how important this corner once was. *(Map by Jeffrey Winslow; Vincent F. Seyfried collection.)*

Ridgewood 117

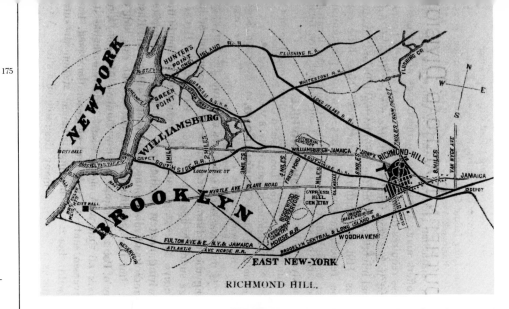

RICHMOND HILL.

RICHMOND HILL

*I*n 1867 the wooded slopes to the east and west of what is now Lefferts Boulevard attracted the attention of Edward Richmond, a landscape architect. He proposed to Albon P. Man, a wealthy New York lawyer, the purchase of the area, then the Lefferts and Welling farms. In 1869 work began on laying out the tract between the Brooklyn and Jamaica Plank Road (Jamaica Avenue) and the Union Turnpike, which received the name Richmond Hill. Streets were laid out, shade trees planted and model homes erected. From 1868 to 1910 the Man family firmly controlled development. In 1895 Richmond Hill became an independent village, with Alrick H. Man, son of Albon, as first president. Development was especially rapid between 1895 and World War I, with hundreds of houses erected north and south of Jamaica Avenue. Richmond Hill, even after a century, retains its fine residential character and suburban flavor.

175. DEVELOPER'S MAP OF RICHMOND HILL, 1872. The marketing of Richmond Hill: the developer's brochure for the auction of lots in 1872. Oliver B. Fowler, an old friend of Albon P. Man, became the agent in charge of selling lots in the new development and used this map to acquaint people with the location of the property. Between April 1869 and the end of 1872 there were regular auctions of lots, complete with free railroad tickets, military bands and free food. (*Vincent F. Seyfried collection.*)

176. LEFFERTS AVENUE NORTH OF HILLSIDE AVENUE, ca. 1905. Lefferts Avenue (now Lefferts Boulevard) was the showpiece street of Richmond Hill. This summer view, heavily shaded by trees planted in the 1870's, shows glimpses of handsome, baronial mansions on big plots; huge porches shaded by awnings mark the front of these typical Victorian houses. The street is spotless and parking problems are far in the future. (*The Queens Borough Public Library.*)

177. HILLSIDE AND LEFFERTS AVE-
NUES, ca. 1905. The massive proportions of
the fine Victorian house on the corner would
challenge the skills of the most energetic
1980's housewife. Cupolas on corners, lunettes
and round windows, balustrades on both
second and third floors and even on the roof
are typical examples of Victorian whimsy;
huge wraparound porches were no less popular in this expansive, confident era before
World War I. *(From a postcard; Vincent F.
Seyfried collection.)*

178. BROOKLYN AND JAMAICA PLANK
ROAD (JAMAICA AVENUE) AT LEF-
FERTS AVENUE, LOOKING EAST, ca.
1906. In this day, before the coming of the
elevated, many of the neighborhood stores
were still wooden frame buildings; the city
enacted a fire code right after 1898 requiring
that all new construction along Jamaica Avenue be of brick or stone like the new building
at the right. The grade crossing in the foreground was eliminated in 1913. *(E. B. Watson
collection)*

179. BROOKLYN AND JAMAICA PLANK
ROAD (JAMAICA AVENUE) AT 116th
STREET, LOOKING EAST, 1906. Beginning about 1900 the occasional farmhouses
along the avenue began to give way to block
after block of buildings like this, with store-
fronts on the ground floor and "flats" or
apartments on the two upper floors. Many of
these brick commercial buildings still stand
through Woodhaven and Richmond Hill. The
elevated line was built along Jamaica Avenue
in 1916, obscuring the buildings but making
the place look very "citified." *(E. B. Watson
collection.)*

180. MYRTLE AVENUE, LOOKING NORTH, AT BROOKLYN AND JAMAICA PLANK ROAD (JAMAICA AVENUE), ca. 1906. This was the best-known street corner in Richmond Hill. Both avenues were originally turnpikes, collecting tolls from users. The Triangle Hotel, still in business today as a restaurant, occupies the corner. The place began as a wayside inn about 1870 and has had a succession of owners through the years. This photo shows the Myrtle Avenue trolley waiting to begin its return trip to Ridgewood. (*Vincent F. Seyfried collection.*)

181. JOHNSON AVENUE (NOW 118th STREET), LOOKING SOUTH FROM THE BROOKLYN AND JAMAICA PLANK ROAD (JAMAICA AVENUE), ca. 1908. Rutted roads were the rule in Richmond Hill at this early period. At the right is old Police Precinct No. 78 and alongside it old Public School 51, built in 1891. Both buildings are long since gone but many private houses along 118th Street are still standing. *(Queens Topographical Bureau collection.)*

182. JACOB RIIS HOUSE, BEECH STREET NEAR CENTRAL AVENUE (LATER 84-41 120th STREET), ca. 1910. Jacob Riis is probably Richmond Hill's most famous citizen. He was born in Denmark in 1849 and came to New York in 1870. He liked to write and became a journalist. In 1877 he became a police reporter and had numerous occasions to tour the slums. Moved by the terrible conditions he witnessed, he wrote powerful articles culminating in several famous books, *How the Other Half Lives, Children of the Poor* and *The Making of an American.* Riis also originated in America the idea of Christmas seals. His Richmond Hill house was demolished in November 1973. *(Queens Topographical Bureau collection.)*

183. LEFFERTS AVENUE, LOOKING NORTH FROM ATLANTIC AVENUE, APRIL 24, 1913. The Disneyland architecture of the Morris Park Hotel on the corner of Atlantic Avenue dominates the scene with its Moorish cupola and half-timbered facade. At the right is Morris Park station. The street, today one of the busiest, is still unpaved and automobiles are rare. *(L.I.R.R. photo; Robert Presbrey collection.)*

182

184. NEAR CLARENCEVILLE STATION, APRIL 24, 1913. Looking north up 111th Street (then Greenwood Avenue) from Atlantic Avenue. The street is still unpaved, horse droppings dot the surface and saloons stand at two of the four corners. The Clarenceville railroad station is at the left; the wooden gates came down when trains passed. (*L.I.R.R. photo; Robert Presbrey collection.*)

185. CLARENCEVILLE STATION, ATLANTIC AVENUE, 1922. Just west of 111th Street, this was the busiest of Richmond Hill's three railroad stations, with heavy commuter traffic. Other stations were at Hillside Avenue and 118th Street (still standing) and at Morris Park (Atlantic Avenue and 120th Street). The local service on Atlantic Avenue was abandoned in 1940 when the tracks were put underground. (*Photo by J. Osborne; Ron Ziel collection.*)

186. STENBERG BROS. AD, 1924. A typical developer's ad of 1924, illustrating the type of house being constructed by the hundreds during the boom years of 1920–30. These are better-class houses, with some attempt made to vary the monotony of construction, plus an alleyway and a garage for each to accommodate the family Model "A" Ford. The high price range of $8,200 to $15,000 limited these houses to upper-middle-class purchasers. (*From* Queenborough *magazine; The Queens Borough Public Library.*)

OVER THREE THOUSAND *of* THESE HOMES

Built by us in Richmond Hill, South, during the last four years

Highly Restricted Residential Section, Fully Improved.   **Prices from $8,200 up to $15,000.**

Homes to be built in Forest Hills Gardens, from $18,000 up, or to order.

OFFICE:

11106 LIBERTY AVENUE   **RICHMOND HILL**

Telephone Richmond Hill 5936

GLENDALE

Glendale lies in the middle of Queens County, bounded roughly by Fresh Pond Road, the Long Island Rail Road, Woodhaven Boulevard and the Interborough Parkway, and is almost surrounded by cemeteries and parklands. Boomed first in 1869 by John Schooley (of Glendale, Ohio, hence the name) and associates, Glendale grew slowly, the last housing developments being completed between the two World Wars and filling the last remaining lands. Glendale today is predominantly German, but with many Irish, Polish, Italian and Yugoslavian families; there are many row houses of World War I vintage, the rest detached one- and two-family houses. The 240-unit Forest Park Crescent Cooperative, twenty stories high, at the eastern end of town, is the only large development. Some knitting mills and a sprinkling of small factories are the only industry. Forest Park, 451 acres of unspoiled woodland, is the glory of Glendale and replaces the old-time open farmlands.

187. LUTHERAN CEMETERY (NEAR ENTRANCE) AT GLENDALE STATION, OCTOBER 3, 1906. At the left is George Gundolf's saloon on Clinton Avenue (now on 70th Avenue at 73rd Street), built in 1891. For a while it became a combination saloon and florist shop. Gundolf's widow Karolina revived the saloon after Prohibition; it is still a bar today. The building at the right, now a residence, was a saloon run by Christian Kirschmann and later Balbina Lorenz, but owned by Joseph Bermel, Borough President of Queens from 1905 through 1907. (L.I.R.R. photo; Ron Ziel collection.)

188. UNITY HALL, 65-02 MYRTLE AVENUE, ca. 1909. This multipurpose structure was built just east of Cypress Hills Street in 1909. It had bowling alleys in the basement, Minnie Peters' saloon on the ground floor and an assembly hall upstairs. For a while Judge Denton held his court here and the saloon became a bicycle shop. Today the Kolping Society uses the second floor, and a bar again occupies the street floor. The columns disappeared during the 1920's. (Robert F. Eisen collection.)

189. LAST MUSTER, ca. 1913. Ivanhoe Park Fire Hook and Ladder Company No. 10 on the east side of Cypress Hills Street opposite 74th Avenue (then Fresh Pond Road at Glasser Street), Glendale. On September 1, 1913, this company and all the other volunteer companies in Queens's 2nd Ward, the old Town of Newtown, were replaced by the New York City Fire Department. This full-dress photo was probably taken to commemorate the last muster of the company before its going out of existence. (Robert F. Eisen collection.)

190. CAROUSEL, FOREST PARK, ca. 1918.
This impressive carousel was built by William
H. Dentzel in Philadelphia. The horses, lions
and simulated-leather saddles were all hand-
carved by Daniel Muller, a master carousel
carver. The horse even has a spear-bearing
Indian carved on his flank. (*Henry Dehls
collection; courtesy of Robert F. Eisen.*)

191. GLENDALE, LOOKING WEST, JUNE 2, 1933. This aerial view was taken by the now-defunct Fairchild Aerial Surveys. The Lutheran Cemetery is at the right. The railroad and Cooper Avenue make an "X" in the middle; Central Avenue is at the top, and 80th Street is in the foreground. Even fifty-five years ago Glendale was well built up. *(Photo by Fairchild Aerial Surveys; Vincent F. Seyfried collection.)*

192. MYRTLE AVENUE AT 68th STREET, FEBRUARY 1950 (LOOKING EAST). *(Photo by Vincent F. Seyfried.)*

193. MYRTLE AVENUE AT 79th LANE, FEBRUARY 1950 (LOOKING EAST). *(Photo by Vincent F. Seyfried.)*

194. MYRTLE AVENUE AT 79th LANE, FEBRUARY 1950 (LOOKING WEST). Much of Glendale today preserves the small-town atmosphere conveyed by these forty-year-old photographs. *(Photo by Vincent F. Seyfried.)*

Glendale 131

CREEDMOOR

The Creedmoor Rifle Range formerly occupied the site of what is now the Creedmoor Psychiatric Center (Creedmoor State Hospital), bounded, approximately, by Hillside Avenue, Winchester Boulevard and the Belt Parkway in Queens Village. The land was deeded to the State in 1872 for use as a rifle range by the New York National Guard. Complaints about drunken guardsmen in the streets of Queens Village and bullets coming too close to neighboring houses induced the state to close the range in 1908 and to turn over the grounds as a site for a state mental hospital in 1910. In the 1870's and '80's international rifle matches were regularly staged here between American and European teams and there was even a rifle developed bearing the Creedmoor name. The grounds accommodated a large clubhouse, a railroad station, extensive butts and a local hotel. Trainloads of reservists from Brooklyn and other parts of Queens used to come here every summer to improve their shooting skills. Some memory of the old Creedmoor range still survives in the names of Musket, Sabre and Range Streets near the site of the former railroad station.

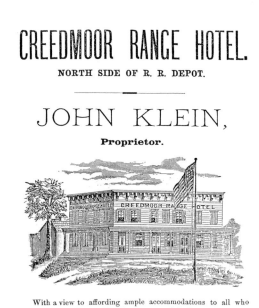

195. AMERICAN INTERNATIONAL RIFLE-MATCH TEAM, JULY 10, 1875. Formal portrait of nine very self-conscious high-ranking reservists, photographed at Creedmoor with their rifles, reamers and sights in July 1875. (*From* Harper's Weekly.)

196. AD OF THE CREEDMOOR RANGE HOTEL, 1877. This ad was run by the Hotel's proprietor, Captain John Klein; the captain was killed when his carriage was upset on July 9, 1879, but his widow carried on until the range closed. (*From an old newspaper; The Queens Borough Public Library.*)

197. THOUSAND-YARD RANGE, CREEDMOOR, 1877. This rare stereoscopic view was taken during the 1877 International Match shoot. The contestant is shooting from a low posture on the ground. (*Photo by Waller and Schrader; J. Rodriguez collection.*)

198. 1877 INTERNATIONAL MATCH, FROM THE REAR. The spectators are protected from the hot July sun under tents and umbrellas. (*Stereoscopic view; J. Rodriguez collection.*)

Creedmoor 133

CREEDMOOR CLUB HOUSE
AND PAVILION.

The Club-House and Pavilion now building at the "Range," and which will be opened on the 15th of May, will, it is claimed by the projectors, supply a much needed requirement at Creedmoor. The establishment has been specially assigned as a head-quarters for the National Rifle Association, Private Rifle Clubs, the National Guardsmen of the State, as well as for those who visit these famous shooting grounds either as contestants or spectators. The management intend to combine all the comforts, conveniences and amusements possible consistent with their present accommodations, and at no late day will add the additional attraction of a First-Class Hotel. One of the prominent features of the present building will be a handsomely-furnished Ladies' Parlor and Retiring Rooms, with proper attendance; and a portion of the extensive Piazza, running the whole length of the building, and from which an unobstructed view of the grounds and the shooting can be obtained, will be exclusively alloted to the accommodation of lady visitors.

The Dining Room will be a large and spacious appartment, and it is intended to make the *cuisine* equal in all respects to the requirements of visitors. Private rooms for Rifle Clubs, and individual lockers for riflemen, will occupy the second floor, and will be one of the features, and add additional life and interest to the place. A number of uniformed boys will be attached to the Pavillion, and be stationed at different parts on the grounds, whose duty it will be to act as messengers and attend to the wants of the shooters and others, and supply refreshments on the field without additional cost.

Croquet, Archery, Lawn Tennis and other outdoor sports will be furnished for ladies ; and the management undertake to provide everything of the best, and at prices which cannot fail to command large and liberal support, and in fact to make Creedmoor a delightful and attractive resort to everybody taking an interest in the National Sport of Rifle Shooting.

GREAT REDUCTION ! RIFLES, SHOT GUNS, REVOLVERS, &c. Send stamp for Illustrated Catalogue, Price List, Treatise, Record, &c., to E. Remington & Sons, 283 Bd'way, N. Y.

199. AD OF THE CREEDMOOR CLUB HOUSE AND PAVILION, 1878. This sizeable clubhouse opened on the Creedmoor grounds on May 15, 1878. The two-story building measured 150 by 50 feet, with a tower at either end. The main saloon was 75 feet long, with capacious dining rooms adjoining it. On the second floor were private rooms for rifle clubs and for contestants staying overnight. *(From an old newspaper; The Queens Borough Public Library.)*

200. BRITISH RIFLE TEAM, 1882. Rare lineup of photos of the visiting team at an international match in 1882. *(The Queens Borough Public Library.)*

BAYSIDE

*B*ayside occupies a northeast corner of Queens, facing the Sound and Little Neck Bay. For most of the nineteenth century it was a quiet farming area; in 1872 the Bayside Land Company began the first real-estate promotion. The high land facing Little Neck Bay was studded with mansions set in parklike surroundings. By 1920 intensive home building was under way and the large estates were broken up. Today apartments and condos are crowding out the older homes and the Belt Parkway has sealed off the waterfront. Crocheron Park and the Oakland Lake area preserve a little of the rural Bayside of yesteryear.

201. BEACH NEAR CROCHERON HOUSE, MAY 1894. For years the best-known place in Bayside was the Crocheron House, overlooking Little Neck Bay at the foot of Crocheron Avenue. This old hotel was the goal of political outings and of bicycle and wagon jaunts and a prime vacation spot for families from New York. The original burned down in 1878 but was rebuilt. In the rear are the carriage sheds where the horses were tethered and fed. In this scene several men are digging for clams along the beach. *(Suffolk County Historical Society collection.)*

202. BELL AVENUE, LOOKING NORTH, JULY 6, 1917. The then-small Bayside shopping area lies just ahead; awnings shade each store and automobiles are already parked along the curbs. America has just entered World War I, and an American flag and Red Cross banner hang over the west side of the street. Now, nearly seventy-five years later, Bell Avenue is Bell Boulevard, and the railroad tracks pass under the street. *(L.I.R.R. photo; Robert Presbrey collection.)*

203. ESTATE AREA, SEEN FROM LITTLE NECK BAY, JUNE 1923. The Bayside Yacht Club is in the foreground, and at the extreme left are the homes of Pearl White, Norma Talmadge and Jim Corbett. Today all the estates are broken up, the area is densely built up and Robert Moses has taken over the whole shoreline for his Belt Parkway. *(Photo by Fairchild Aerial Surveys; Vincent F. Seyfried collection.)*

204. BELL AVENUE FROM 41st AVENUE, LOOKING SOUTH, JUNE 1927. The business section is growing: two-story buildings are making their appearance, signs are becoming conspicuous and there are the beginnings of a parking problem. *(From* Queensborough *magazine; The Queens Borough Public Library.)*

205. HARWAY HOUSE, OCTOBER 11, 1933. The Bayside that was: the Harway house at 27th Avenue and 216th Street. Victorian Gothic houses were always a rarity in Queens, and this is one of the best examples. Bayside was a favorite of wealthy New Yorkers in the nineteenth century because it offered an abundance of sites overlooking Little Neck Bay. The Harway Mansion succumbed to the wreckers in 1938. *(The Queens Borough Public Library.)*

206. LOOKING NORTH INTO 222nd AND 223rd STREETS FROM THE GRAND CENTRAL PARKWAY, 1945. The houses here are typical of the suburban-style upper-middle-class housing of eastern Queens. Handsome Tudors and English cottages stand on quiet streets, with some of the original trees intact. *(The Queens Borough Public Library.)*

205

HOLLIS

Hollis is the brainchild of Frederick W. Dunton, last Supervisor of the Town of Jamaica. In 1885 he and his backers bought two farms and laid out the village of Hollis. By 1910 there were 130 houses within a half-mile of the station; most were Victorian-style houses, with a few surviving farmhouses. In 1906 Hollis Park Gardens, a development from 191st to 195th Street, catering to the affluent, began building high-class houses. Beginning in 1922 many new streets were laid out between Hillside and Jamaica Avenues, and tract houses were put up by the hundreds. By World War II Hollis was a completely built-up community. Today the neighborhood streets still retain their residential suburban quality, though many of the 80- to 100-year-old houses have yielded to garden apartments.

207. MAP OF HOLLIS, ca. 1902. Bird's-eye views like this were very popular around 1900 before aerial photography was perfected. This developer's map shows Hollis about 1902, most of the settlement being concentrated between Woodhull and Jamaica Avenues. Many streets have been laid out south of the railroad and also in Holliswood, but houses are few. Very few of these original turn-of-the-century structures remain today. (*The Queens Borough Public Library.*)

208. REAL-ESTATE AD, MAY 13, 1906. A full-page ad in the *New-York Daily Tribune*, booming "Hollis Terrace," a development on 104th Avenue and the streets intersecting it. Note the many claimed advantages of residence in Hollis; none of the pictures show the actual property, and the station name has been retouched.

209. HOLLIS PARK GARDENS, 1910. The corner of Hollis and Belleview Avenues (now 89th Avenue and 190th Street), looking east. Old Public School 35 and the Lutheran Church are visible in the background. Many of the decorative masonry pillars bearing the monogram of the development are still standing. (*Real-estate-company brochure; Vincent F. Seyfried collection.*)

207

HOLLISWOOD.
THE GEM OF LONG ISLAND!

209

HOLLIS 141

212

210. HILLSIDE AVENUE AT CHEROKEE AVENUE (NOW 196th STREET), LOOKING EAST, 1914. Is this an accident or just a conflict over a parking space? The decorative pillars marking Hollis Park Gardens on either side of the avenue are clearly visible. The avenue, so choked with traffic today, is here almost empty—no cars and no pedestrians; no wonder the mounted policeman looks bored! *(Photo by Frederick J. Weber; The Queens Borough Public Library.)*

211. HILLSIDE AVENUE AT 188th STREET, LOOKING WEST, 1917. A sign of changing times is that the carriage shed of the Hollis Arms Hotel at the right is now occupied by a one-pump gas station. Today the north side of the street (right) is completely lined with apartment houses, and the subway terminal at 179th Street has enormously increased auto and bus traffic. *(Photo by Frederick J. Weber; The Queens Borough Public Library.)*

212. JAMAICA AVENUE AT 184th STREET, FEBRUARY 26, 1926. One of the enduring scenes of old Hollis. Before the coming of the storm sewers, water regularly poured down all the streets during every heavy rain and accumulated on Jamaica Avenue at this low point in the road at 184th Street. Cars and trucks risking the passage always lost power and were marooned until the water went down. The trolley company is using a special high-wheeled rig at the right to tow a car through the "lake," ferrying passengers from one side to the other. The factory building at the right is still in use. *(Photo by Frederick J. Weber; The Queens Borough Public Library.)*

Hollis 143

215

213. FARMERS AVENUE (BOULEVARD), LOOKING WEST ALONG JAMAICA AVENUE, MARCH 1, 1928. Jamaica Avenue between Jamaica and Queens Village was increased in width from 70 to 100 feet in 1930, necessitating the moving back of all these buildings; the trolley gave way to buses on November 25, 1933. The old tollgate of the Hempstead and Jamaica Plank Road occupied the center of this picture until October 4, 1895, when Jamaica Avenue was declared a free road. The Creo Bros. hardware store had been Samuel Durland's grocery store in the 1870's and '80's. The stores with apartments above were all built in 1921–22, when Hollis had begun to grow. *(Photo by Frederick J. Weber; The Queens Borough Public Library.)*

214. JAMAICA AVENUE AT FARMERS AVENUE (BOULEVARD), LOOKING EAST, MARCH 1, 1928. A primitive diner occupied the triangle for a few years, but the city later planted trees on the site. The turreted building was the main grocery store of Hollis till its demolition in 1930. The building boom of the 1920's is evident in Riccardo's real-estate office and big billboard at the right and the rival real-estate office at the left offering one- and two-family houses. Note the price of gasoline in 1928—15 cents a gallon! *(Photo by Frederick J. Weber; The Queens Borough Public Library.)*

215. JAMAICA AVENUE, LOOKING EAST FROM 192nd STREET, JULY 1931. This is the heart of the shopping district. All the stores are still standing today, but the little Hollis Theatre at the right, opened in 1925, has long since vanished. The effect of the road widening of 1930 is evident here; the new curb line is about twenty-four feet beyond the old one, but the addition remained unpaved and unused for a few years. *(Photo by Frederick J. Weber; The Queens Borough Public Library.)*

Hollis   145

NORTH BEACH

North Beach lives today only as a pleasant memory in the minds of older Queens residents. Launched in 1886 as a joint venture of William Steinway, the piano manufacturer, and George Ehret, the brewmaster (Hell Gate beer), North Beach was an attempt to provide a people's playground on Queens soil not only for the local inhabitants of Astoria and Long Island City but for the working classes of Manhattan and the Bronx. First called Bowery Bay Beach, it was renamed North Beach in 1891. The resort advertised itself as a family playground, offering food and drink, bathing, entertainment, carousels, Ferris Wheels, chutes and other rides, picnic grounds and several hotels for extended stays. North Beach was, in a real sense, the Coney Island of Queens and flourished until Prohibition, World War I austerity and changing tastes ended its popularity. In 1929 the land was sold as a site for Glenn Curtiss (North Beach) Airport, later developed by the city into La Guardia Field. Today, concrete runways completely cover the former playground.

---

216. JACKSON'S MILL POND, ca. 1880. It's hard to believe but today this is the entrance to La Guardia Field! The primitive road crossing the dam is now 94th Street and the millpond in the foreground is the site of the Grand Central Parkway. The old mill, known successively as Kip's, Fish's and Jackson's Mill, and powered by a large undershot wheel, used to grind wheat and corn for the inhabitants of north Queens till about 1870. This view looks northeast to Flushing Bay (seen in the rear) and was photographed within a year or two of 1880. (*Queens Historical Society collection.*)

217. GRAND PIER, STEAMBOAT LAND-ING, 1892. Regular lines of boats brought pleasure seekers from 99th and 130th Streets in New York and 138th Street in the Bronx and from College Point. Grand Pier was 300 feet long and 120 feet wide; on it was North Beach Pavilion, long operated by Paul Steinhagen and Julius Kelterborn, and accommodating 2,000 people. Lunches were served by attentive waiters, and a band played lively music. (*Photo by Paul Geipel; Queens Historical Society.*)

217

218

220

218. BATHING BEACH, 1892. The bathing beach at North Beach alongside one of the sightseeing piers in 1892. There are ropes in the water for bathers to hang on to and floodlights on the posts illuminating the scene for night enjoyment. As is usual in pictures of this period, the great majority of the bathers are men and boys; the great difficulties of getting into and out of the complicated dress of the day tended to discourage women from freely enjoying public bathing at the beaches. *(Photo by Paul Geipel; Queens Historical Society.)*

219. GEORGE W. KREMER'S SILVER SPRING CAROUSEL, 1898. This impressive carousel was located at the waterfront at about 80th Street, near the Silver Spring Swimming Pool. Twenty-four medallions of the presidents alternating with literary scenes decorated the carousel roofline; below, horses, camels and oversize dogs provided rides for the small fry. Several such carousels, along with Ferris Wheels, chutes and scenic railways, provided a Coney Island–like atmosphere. *(From a brochure; Dora Geipel collection.)*

220. FERRIS WHEEL, ca. 1900. A quiet day in winter. This wheel is unusually large and high, with eighteen gondolas. Its whole weight is borne by the right-hand anchorage; the left supports the revolving gear. The street in the foreground is Grand Boulevard. *(The Queens Borough Public Library.)*

221

224

Sour would you like to slide down here Josie.

Shooting the Chutes, North Beach, L. I.

222

221. "OLD SWIMMING HOLE," ca. 1900. Boys enjoying the summertime in their own way and in their own private swimming hole in the "good old days" around 1900. The wooded shoreline along the East River from Astoria to Bowery Bay provided numerous secluded nooks for informal bathing. The Consolidated Edison plant now owns and occupies most of this shoreline. *(Photo by Paul Geipel; Queens Historical Society.)*

222. "SHOOTING THE CHUTES," ca. 1905. The chutes were one of the main attractions at North Beach. Patrons climbed into a small railcar, then hurtled down the incline and shot out into the waters of the lake below. On this day an aerialist is performing for the crowd by riding down a wire, supported only by a bit held between his teeth. *(From a postcard; Vincent F. Seyfried collection.)*

223. DANCE-HALL INTERIOR, ca. 1905. Interior of the dancing pavilion of Henry Daufkirch's Bay View Hotel at North Beach fronting on the Sound. This huge combination of hotel, beer garden and dancing pavilion was typical of the many at North Beach during its golden age, 1891–1920. Thousands of New Yorkers came here to escape the heat of the tenements and to enjoy a day in the open at minimal cost—10 cents on the ferry and 5 cents for a glass of beer; a lunch cost 25 cents and a full-course meal 75 cents. Prohibition killed North Beach and resort hotels like Daufkirch's. *(Phyllis Daufkirch Ritz collection.)*

224. SCENIC RAILWAY, ca. 1912. There were two scenic railways at North Beach; this view shows a close-up of the riding strips and guide timbers for the car during a midwinter maintenance check. Rides like this, along with beer halls, shows, games of chance and fast-food outlets for ice cream, soft drinks and hot food provided entertainment for the daily throngs of pleasure seekers that converged here via steamboat, ferry and trolley. *(The Queens Borough Public Library.)*

150   North Beach

JAMAICA BAY

J amaica Bay for most of the nineteenth century and the first decade of the twentieth was a watery vastness dotted here and there by odd-shaped islets called hassocks that rose out of the sea a few inches at low tide and disappeared from sight again at high water. Vast fields of waving salt-meadow grass stretched to the horizon, and narrow channels snaked their serpentine way through the primeval wilderness. Old maps of the bay are dotted with strange and exotic names whose origins are lost to history: Big Egg Marsh, Ruler's Bar Hassock, The Raunt, Conch's Hole, Goose Creek, Jo Co's Marsh, etc. The earliest access to the meadows was the Rockaway Turnpike, which skirted the edge of the marshland through Springfield, Hook Creek and Cedarhurst. The coming of the trolley in 1896 opened the meadows for boating and fishing. The first incursion into the bay itself was the building of the five-mile trestle of the New York, Woodhaven and Rockaway Railroad (later absorbed into the Long Island Rail Road) in 1880. Fishing stations were built where the rails crossed hassocks and, down to World War I, waterside hotels, saloons and shacks renting rowboats and bait prospered. The closing of Jamaica Bay in 1916 to both shellfishing and bathing because of advancing pollution put an end to a pleasant era wherein the bay served as a playground for the people of Brooklyn as well as Queens.

225. DREDGER AT WORK, NEAR ROCKAWAY TURNPIKE, ca. 1895. A sight rarely photographed: a turn-of-the-century dredger chews its slow way through the marshland alongside Rockaway Turnpike, which can be seen in the background by the line of telephone poles. The channels helped to drain off stagnant water and cut down on mosquitoes by allowing the tides to flush the meadows. Channels were also cut in meandering bodies of water like Hook Creek to create straight courses for boaters. (*Photo by Dan Smith; The Queens Borough Public Library.*)

226

228

226. FISHERMAN, JAMAICA BAY, ca. 1900.
Life in a fishing shack on Jamaica Bay re-
volved around boat rowing, setting crab
traps, eeling and just plain lazing on the dock.
The man emptying his traps betrays his
landlubber origins by working in a white
shirt, tie, celluloid collar and hat. *(Photo by
Dan Smith; The Queens Borough Public
Library.)*

227. DOMESTIC SCENE, MEADOW-
MERE, ca. 1900. A rarely photographed
domestic scene—a woman doing the wash on
the porch of one of the summer shacks at
Meadowmere alongside Hook Creek. A
summer vacation in a fishing shack may have
offered fun and recreation to a man and his
sons, with daily opportunities for swimming
and fishing, but for the wife it was the same
old round of preparing meals, washing and
cleaning. Once an hour a trolley car heading
for Jamaica came along Rockaway Turnpike,
marked by the line of telephone poles in the
background. *(Photo by Dan Smith; The
Queens Borough Public Library.)*

228. SPRINGFIELD DOCK, ca. 1900. Small
summer colonies like this one sprang up at the
mouth of several creeks emptying into
Jamaica Bay. In construction, the houses
could be as substantial as those on land, but
they had to be built on piles because of the
mucky soil and flooding during storms; fresh
water had to come from a community pump,
and outhouses relied on the flush action of the
tides. Rowboats supplied all the transportation, and swimming and boating were always
available. *(The Queens Borough Public
Library.)*

SPRINGFIELD DOCK, L.I.

Station at Broad Channel, N. Y.

Drawbridge at Broad Channel Rockaway

229. CRAB FISHING AT MEADOWMERE, ca. 1900. Meadowmere was a tiny collection of houses built in a loop of Hook Creek at the Nassau County line. The Rockaway Turnpike in the rear was the sole access to this remote settlement. *(Photo by Dan Smith; The Queens Borough Public Library.)*

230. CORNELL CREEK, OCTOBER 24, 1901. Sunset on the marshes. The photo captures very well the vastness of the watery wasteland that was Jamaica Bay a century ago. An isolated boathouse or fishing shack perched on piles was the only sign of civilization in an infinity of grassland and watercourses. The scene is near Three-Mile Mill, at the mouth of Cornell Creek, the stream from Baisley's Pond. *(Photo by W. R. Case; The Queens Borough Public Library.)*

231. BROAD CHANNEL STATION, ca. 1905. Broad Channel, the only remaining community in Jamaica Bay (it was formerly the largest and by far the most developed of a number of fishing villages on islands in the Bay), is situated on Big Egg Marsh. Cross Bay Boulevard (built in 1925) is now the lifeline of the community, and 22 short cross streets intersect it. For years the residents rented their home sites from the city but several years ago won the right to buy the land under their houses. The Long Island Rail Road station shown here was at the eastern edge of town. *(From a postcard; Vincent F. Seyfried collection.)*

232. BROAD CHANNEL DRAWBRIDGE, ca. 1905. This view of the Long Island Rail Road drawbridge looks northeast from Hammels Avenue (now Beach 85th Street), Rockaway. The bridge was pivoted in the center and swung sideways to allow boats to go through. The railroad trestle was considered an engineering marvel when it was built in 1880, and many persons rode it for the novelty of going five miles out to sea in a railroad coach. The train in this photo is a Brooklyn Rapid Transit train. These trains were run over Long Island Rail Road tracks from 1898 to 1917. The "A" and "C" subway trains now follow the same route, but extensive filling has shortened the overwater ride by two-thirds. *(From a postcard; Vincent F. Seyfried collection.)*

Jamaica Bay 157

FOREST HILLS

Forest Hills began in 1904, when Cord Meyer, Jr., heir to his father's sugar-refining fortune, bought six hundred acres of land along Queens Boulevard in an area then known as Whitepot. Over the next three years streets were graded and a few houses built. When Penn Station opened in 1910 and the Long Island Rail Road electrified its line through Forest Hills and built the existing station, Forest Hills became easily accessible. In 1909 Cord Meyer sold one hundred acres south of the railroad to the Sage Foundation, which commenced laying out Forest Hills Gardens. Both communities grew slowly, adding churches, schools and stores. When the West Side Tennis Club came to Forest Hills in 1914 and built a stadium for its matches, Forest Hills became known nationally. By 1925, 9,500 people were living here, attracted by the high quality of the housing, the suburban atmosphere and the good transportation. The first apartment house came in 1917, followed by many more along Queens Boulevard in the 1920's. Today Forest Hills is one of the premier residential neighborhoods of Queens, with its private streets and well-maintained houses reflecting suburban living at its best.

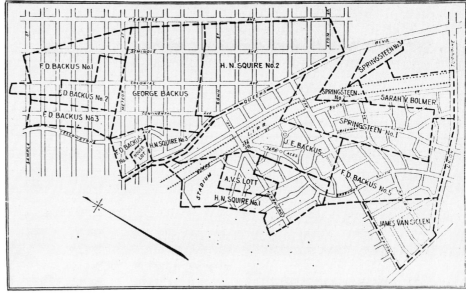

234

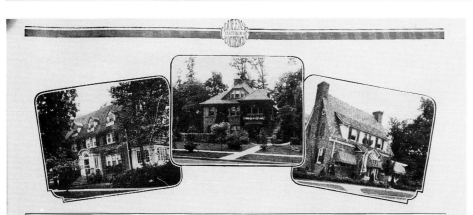

236

233. HOFFMAN (NOW QUEENS) BOULEVARD, LOOKING EAST, 1903. It is almost impossible to believe that this scene is of Queens Boulevard looking east from 69th Avenue (then Livingston Street) in 1903. The city was just getting around to installing street lights, telephone poles and a few catch basins through a sparsely settled farm country. The street surface in the photo is largely muddy ruts, and empty fields stretch out to the horizon. *(Long Island Savings Bank collection.)*

234. MAP OF FOREST HILLS, ca. 1917. How Forest Hills was put together: sixteen different farms were assembled like a jigsaw puzzle to create a new community. The Backus farms had been truck gardens producing produce for the New York market; tenant farmers tilled the other properties until displaced by home-building operations. *(From* Queensborough *magazine; The Queens Borough Public Library.)*

235. "VILLAGE GREEN," SOUTH OF THE RAILROAD STATION, ca. 1920. Arched passageways lead to the station platform at the left and to the Inn just out of sight at the right. In the center is the clock tower and the octagon business block. Burns Street appears at the left and Greenway Terrace at the right. *(From a postcard; Vincent F. Seyfried collection.)*

236. HOUSES, FOREST HILLS GARDENS, 1921. An ad of the Sage Foundation, which pioneered Forest Hills Gardens, showing views of some representative houses. The company, named after Mrs. Russell Sage, who financed the project, states its character and aims very clearly in this ad. Forest Hills has retained its character and suburban charm to a high degree over the past seventy years, even with the coming of the subway and the commercialization of Queens Boulevard. *(From* Queensborough *magazine; The Queens Borough Public Library.)*

237

240

239

237. AERIAL VIEW OF THE HEART OF FOREST HILLS, LOOKING NORTH-EAST, 1924. Apartment buildings are clustered around the railroad station but the wooded central sector is less than half built up and the foreground not at all. The tennis stadium is at the left. *(Photo by Fairchild Aerial Surveys; from* Queensborough *magazine; The Queens Borough Public Library.)*

238. DEVELOPER'S AD, JANUARY 1928. The Continental Apartments as they appeared on completion in January 1928. Five different sizes of apartments were available at rents that now seem unreal. The low-profile, garden-style apartment building was designed to complement, not overwhelm, the private homes in the community, and attention to architectural detail and extensive landscaping contributed to this objective. *(From* Queensborough *magazine; The Queens Borough Public Library.)*

239. KELVIN APARTMENTS, CONTINENTAL AVENUE AND JEWEL STREET (108th STREET AND JEWEL AVENUE), JUNE 1928. The Kelvin Apartments are typical of the smaller, low-rise apartment houses built in the 1920's with a conscious effort toward handsome architectural effect. Note the varied roofline, cluster chimneys, concealed fire escapes, private-home-like eight-over-eight windows and classical cornices. *(From* Queensborough *magazine; The Queens Borough Public Library.)*

240. WEST SIDE TENNIS CLUB STADIUM, AUGUST 8, 1931. A game in progress. The club came here in 1914 because it was being crowded out of its Manhattan courts by apartment builders and wanted unlimited acreage in the country to expand. From 1918 on the National Tennis Tournaments were held here annually, and many of today's prominent stars got their start here. The elaborate Tudor-style clubhouse is at the rear, and the Forest Hills Inn looms up in the background. *(The Queens Borough Public Library.)*

Forest Hills 161

241

242

241. GREENWAY NORTH FROM MID-
DLEMAY CIRCLE, ca. 1940. A typical scene
in Forest Hills Gardens. The Sage Foundation, under Grosvenor Atterbury and John
Almy Tompkins as supervising architects,
strove to create the atmosphere of an English
country village. The thatched-roof effect on
many of the houses and the half-timbered
facades contribute to this look, as also the
front gardens. *(From* Queensborough *magazine; The Queens Borough Public Library.)*

242. QUEENS BOULEVARD, LOOKING
EAST, JULY 1971. This photo was taken
from the roof of the apartment building at
number 104-20. The changes that seventy
years have brought about are almost beyond
belief. (See photo 233, above.) The boulevard
has been widened to 200 feet, the widest
thoroughfare in all New York City, and the
density of population rivals that of Manhattan. The subway line under the street (with
"E," "F," "G" and "R" trains) carries more
passengers than any other line on the transit
system. *(The Queens Borough Public
Library.)*

COOLEST PLACE IN GREATER
NEW YORK

HOTEL HOWARD

HOWARD LANDING
Jamaica Bay, Long Island

AMERICAN AND EUROPEAN PLANS
AT CITY PRICES

All Modern Improvements, Electric Lights, and a
Children's Playground of 200 Acres, including
Baseball.

Bathing and Boating.   *Boats to Let.*
Bait Furnished.

THE FISHERMAN'S PARADISE

L. A. W.
FISH DINNERS TO OUTING PARTIES A SPECIALTY

To Cyclers: We are officially an L. A. W. Hotel, eleven miles from the Fountain, and can be reached
by way of Glenmore Avenue and South Road, or Jamaica Avenue and Woodhaven
Avenue (Lane) to our 2-mile cycle path at Aqueduct Railroad Station to Hotel.

FREE FERRY FROM HOWARD LANDING
(Flag Station), where Brooklyn Union L trains pass frequently; also, L. I. R. R. trains from Long Island
City and Flatbush Avenue stop if conductor is notified.

OPEN ALL WINTER

85

HOWARD
BEACH

H oward Beach, an all-residential community only 25 blocks wide and 9 blocks long, is sharply defined by its natural boundaries: the Belt Parkway on the north, Spring Creek Park on the west, JFK Airport on the east and Jamaica Bay on the south. William J. Howard, a Brooklyn glove manufacturer, acquired much of the land in the 1890's and began extensive development in 1908. Hawtree Creek had long been bordered by fishing shacks built by Brooklyn families for summer boating and fishing. From 1908 to 1914 sand was pumped over the meadows, streets were laid out and houses erected. Hawtree and Shellbank Basins were dug out to create a Venice-like community which grew rapidly in the 1920's and '30's. By 1935 there were 510 houses; in the 1950's and 60's, the west side of Cross Bay Boulevard was developed. Cross Bay Boulevard (built 1924) and the subway (opened June 1956) are Howard Beach's links to the rest of Queens.

243. HOTEL HOWARD, 1899. How it all started: William J. Howard, a Brooklyn manufacturer of kid gloves made from angora goat skins, built the Hotel Howard in 1899 at the end of a long dock that jutted well out into Jamaica Bay at the foot of what is now 98th Street. Behind the hotel were eighteen rental cottages stretched along the boardwalk. To the right was another long boardwalk leading to a narrow station platform on the Long Island Rail Road trestle. The boardwalk, cottages and hotel burned down in a spectacular fire on the night of October 23, 1907. *(From a periodical advertisement; Vincent F. Seyfried collection.)*

244. HAWTREE BASIN, LOOKING NORTHWEST, MAY 27, 1912. Newly filled land along the banks of Hawtree Basin, an artificial canal dredged to provide home owners with backyard boating facilities. The community was then known as Ramblersville. *(L.I.R.R. photo; The Queens Borough Public Library.)*

245

246

245. JUNCTION OF HAWTREE BASIN
AND OLD HAWTREE CREEK, MAY 27,
1912. The way of life shown here has almost
completely disappeared. These summertime
shacks used for weekend boating and fishing
enjoyment have given way to blocks of year-
round houses and a large, well-established
community. (L.I.R.R. photo; Robert Presbrey collection.)

246. HEAD OF HAWTREE CREEK, JUNE
1928. A very few of these ancient shacks still
border the banks of Hawtree Creek; before
1914, when Howard Beach Estates began to
develop the present-day community, this was
the whole community, which then bore the
name Ramblersville. The Long Island Rail
Road station and a train appear in the background. (From an old newspaper; The
Queens Borough Public Library.)

164   Howard Beach

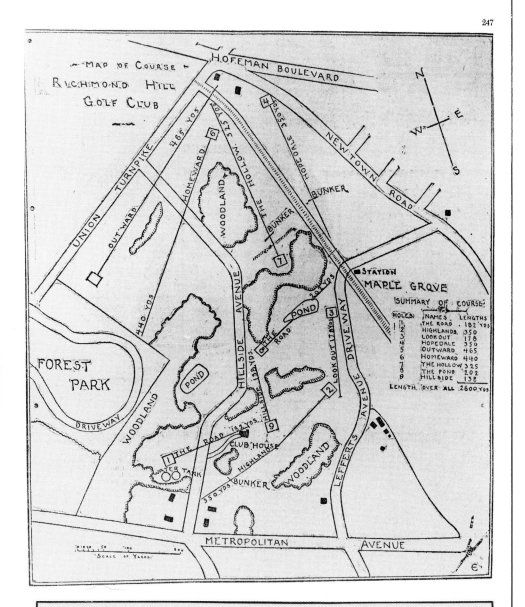

247

Kew Gardens

(Fifteen minutes from Pennsylvania Station)

THE most attractive section of the restricted residential park of 400 acres extending from Richmond Hill station over the hills to Kew station with upwards of 100 trains daily.

Its natural beauty, artistic development and location on the summit of Long Island looking over Forest Hills to the Sound on the north and Richmond Hill to the sea on the south, its frontage of a mile on Forest Park and the fact that it enjoys all the comforts of the established community of Richmond Hill with its churches, schools, clubs and social activities, ensure permanence as a social centre, and rapid increase of land values. Plots and attractive new houses are offered at moderate prices and on convenient terms to acceptable purchasers only.

KEW GARDENS CORPORATION

Telephone Greeley 5250   MARBRIDGE BUILDING   34th Street and Broadway

248

KEW GARDENS

Kew Gardens began as Hopedale, the name of the railroad station for Maple Grove Cemetery in 1875. The present Kew Gardens area was for years the Richmond Hill Golf Club, laid out by Alrick H. Man in the 1890's. When the Long Island Rail Road relocated its Main Line in 1908–09, the golf course was closed and the land was sold to developers, who named the place "Kew," after the London botanical garden. The word "Gardens" was added in 1910 in imitation of Forest Hills Gardens. All the original construction in the area was given over to private homes, but in the 1920's the section near Queens Boulevard began building up with apartment houses. Today, Kew Gardens is one of the best and most expensive residential areas in Queens, full of fine, well-maintained houses on quiet, tree-lined streets.

247. RICHMOND HILL GOLF CLUB, 1906. Kew Gardens as it looked in 1906—a nine-hole golf course with assorted ponds and patches of woodland. When the railroad relocation cut the course in half in 1908, it was decided to sell the course and develop it into a prime residential area. (From the Brooklyn Daily Eagle.)

248. DEVELOPER'S AD, 1915. A 1915 ad of the original developers, the Kew Gardens Corporation. The developers stress the original landscaping, the high terrrain, the nearness and availability of Forest Park and the good transportation. This view is on Lefferts Avenue (Boulevard) and shows the style of large villa still to be seen there today. (From Queensborough magazine; The Queens Borough Public Library.)

165

250

251

249. QUEENS BOULEVARD AT UNION TURNPIKE, LOOKING SOUTHEAST, 1921. The Kew Gardens Inn at the left had just been built on this prominent corner opposite Queens Borough Hall as a suburban hotel for residential and transient guests. The 1920's rates offered one room and bath with meals for 40 dollars a week or two rooms and bath with meals for 85 dollars. The building later became a private hospital. It was torn down in the late 1970's. (*Photo by Frederick J. Weber; The Queens Borough Public Library.*)

250. SHELLBALL APARTMENTS, JANUARY 1929. This typical Kew Gardens apartment house of the 1920's, on Talbot Street and Lefferts Boulevard, opened in the month of this photograph. There are 108 suites in this nine-story complex, a greater density than in the low-rise apartment buildings in Forest Hills. More recently, as land has become increasingly scarce in Queens, the newest apartment buildings of the 1970's and '80's have tended to be more and more massive and multistoried. (*From* Queensborough *magazine; The Queens Borough Public Library.*)

251. "CIVIC VIRTUE," ca. 1941. "Civic Virtue" stands outside Borough Hall in Kew Gardens and has been a source of controversy since sculptor Frederick MacMonnies created it in 1922. The heroic, seventeen-foot-high, ten-ton Georgia-marble statue is supposed to represent Civic Virtue triumphing over two female figures symbolizing Vice and Corruption. Feminists early objected to this characterization of woman as evil and treacherous, while others ridiculed the muscular naked youth as "Fat Boy" and "Tough Guy." The model was New York City Police officer and Olympic Gold Medal winner George Lorz. The statue stood in City Hall Park from 1922 to 1941, and was exiled by Mayor La Guardia and rededicated at Queens Borough Hall on October 7, 1941. (*The Queens Borough Public Library.*)

Kew Gardens   167

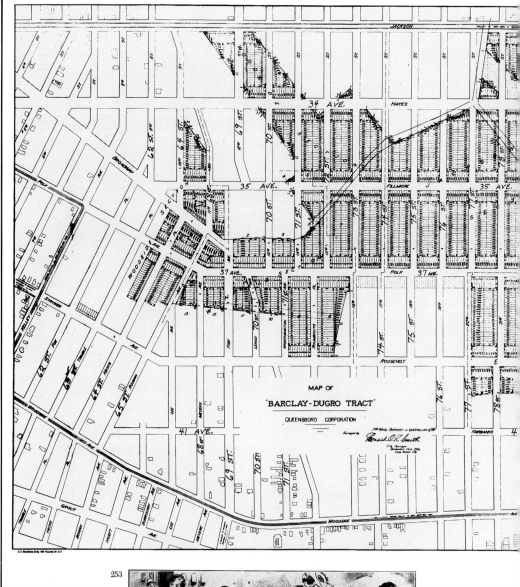

MAP OF
"BARCLAY-DUGRO TRACT"
QUEENSBORO CORPORATION

JACKSON HEIGHTS

J ackson Heights was the creation of the Queensboro Corporation, a syndicate of men prominent in real-estate, business and financial circles. Incorporated in 1908, the firm began actively acquiring real estate in 1909 along a then-existing colonial highway, Trains Meadow Road, between Woodside and Corona. The first acquisitions came cheaply at $6,500 per acre but by 1918 when the last pieces were purchased, the price had risen to $18,500 an acre; all in all, the company purchased 28 different farm properties. The first street laid out was 82nd Street in 1910, followed by the blocks on either side. Between 1910 and 1914 the company built one- and two-family brick houses; beginning in 1914 the first apartments went up. After World War I larger apartment houses were constructed in rapid succession in every year down to the Depression. Tenants in the beginning had to submit references for social compatibility and financial soundness. The company donated land for a community church, St. Joan's and St. Mark's, and built a golf course for its tenants. The Queensboro Corporation was the first real-estate developer in the United States to build garden apartments and the first, beginning in 1920, to introduce cooperative housing to its apartment tenants.

254

An Ideal Home —
A Sound Investment

A Tenant-Owned Garden Apartment at

Jackson Heights

Where more than a thousand families
now own Garden Apartments Homes.

AN IDEAL HOME—because of the location of
Jackson Heights, in the City of New York, Borough
of Queens, East of the midtown section of Manhattan, 22 minutes via the I. R. T. and B. R. T. Subways;
also because of the restrictions which are the foundation on which the existing living and social standards have been established.

AN IDEAL HOME—because of the attractiveness
of the spacious and unique Garden Courts, the safety
and happiness of the children's playgrounds, and the
easy accessibility of the Jackson Heights Golf
Course, Tennis Courts and other recreational facilities.

A SOUND INVESTMENT—first, because of the
reduction of rent to "cost"; second, because of the
erection of a tangible asset; third, because of the
availability of a Tenant-Ownership contract as collateral security; fourth, because of the production
of Garden Apartments on a wholesale basis at the
lowest possible cost consistent with the most modern
designing and construction methods; fifth, because
of the control of 100 City blocks by the Queensboro
Corporation; sixth, because Jackson Heights is the
most highly restricted residential Garden Apartment
Section in New York City, where values are firmly
established on a sound foundation.

A SOUND INVESTMENT—because of the millions
invested in land and buildings by the Queensboro
Corporation, prominent financial institutions, building concerns and the thousand or so prominent New
York City professional and business men who now
are Tenant-Owners of Apartments.

REDUCE YOUR RENT TO "COST" by paying only
your pro-rata share of the cost of operating the
building, annually.

YOUR PRESENT RENT will buy a Garden Apartment if you are paying $150 to $250 a month; small
initial payment; balance same as rent. **Visit Jackson
Heights To-day!**

Jackson Heights

New Elevator Garden Apartment Homes

| Tenant-Ownership Plan | 5 to 7 Rooms—2 to 3 Baths | |
| Liberal Terms | Larger suites to suit your requirements | Social and Business References Required |

The Queensboro Corporation 50 East 42nd St.

Take Subway to Grand Central, transfer to QUEENSBORO SUBWAY (Corona Line) to 25th St.-Jackson Heights Station—Office Opposite Station
By Motor—59th St. via Queensboro Bridge, Jackson Ave. to 25th St.

252. "BARCLAY-DUGRO TRACT," JANUARY 19, 1911. Land holdings of the Queensboro Corporation in January 1911, showing properties in Woodside, Jackson Heights and Elmhurst, mostly between Northern Boulevard (then Jackson Avenue) and Roosevelt Avenue. The company purchased 50 or more acres in 1911 and 1912, ending up with over 350 acres of land extending from 64th Street to 92nd Street. *(From a brochure; Vincent F. Seyfried collection.)*

253. QUEENSBORO CORPORATION AD, MAY 1917. This newspaper ad dramatized the pleasures of living in a garden apartment in Jackson Heights and the low rent for four-, five- and six-room apartments. Note the strong emphasis on socially inclined tenants and social life; bowling, tennis and basketball are all available. *(Vincent F. Seyfried collection.)*

254. QUEENSBORO CORPORATION AD, 1923. An ad of 1923 plugging cooperative-apartment investment, with persuasive arguments, both social and financial. Note the caution at lower right: "Social and Business References Required"; this was an effort on the part of the Queensboro Corporation to create a homogeneous community whose members would have as much in common as possible. *(From a newspaper; Vincent F. Seyfried collection.)*

Jackson Heights 169

255. QUEENSBORO CORPORATION OFFICES, MAY 1929. The Corporation's handsome English Tudor–style executive and general office building on 82nd Street at 37th Avenue as it looked in 1929. *(From a brochure; The Queens Borough Public Library.)*

256, 257. "CHATEAU" AND "CAMBRIDGE COURT," MAY 1929. Two views of garden-apartment buildings at Jackson Heights. The yards, formal gardens landscaped by the famous Olmsted Brothers firm, skillfully combined shrubbery and open spaces. Benches were available for strollers. Playgrounds and garages were provided at the edges of the development. *(From a brochure; The Queens Borough Public Library.)*

258. "ENGLISH GARDEN HOMES," MAY 1929. The last type of housing constructed just before the Depression—single-family "English Garden Homes" on the east side of 86th Street between 34th and 35th Avenues. Depending on the amount of inside equipment and luxury, these brick houses sold for $22,500 to $36,000 in 1929, three to four times the price of typical frame houses elsewhere in Queens. *(From a brochure; The Queens Borough Public Library.)*

259. NORTHERN BOULEVARD, LOOK-
ING EAST TOWARD 82nd STREET, SEP-
TEMBER 13, 1933. The main shopping dis-
trict of Jackson Heights. The apartment
house at the right, erected in 1914, was the
first garden-apartment building built by the
Queensboro Corporation. The Boulevard
Theatre, the first theater in Jackson Heights,
is visible just ahead. (Photo by Frederick J.
Weber; The Queens Borough Public Library.)

INDEX

This index lists persons (including photographers), businesses, organizations, buildings, constructions, monuments, statues, squares and parks mentioned in the text, including the captions to the illustrations. Streets, neighborhoods, rivers and other sites are not included. The numbers used are those of pages, not individual illustrations.